GLOBETROTTER™

Wildlife Guide

MALAYSIA

NEW
HOLLAND

Wildlife Guide
MALAYSIA

Helen Oon

CONTENTS

CHAPTER ONE:

Planning your trip	8
The Essential Survival Kit	8
The Country	10
The Enchanting Forest	10
Types of Forest	11
River Deep, Mountain High	16
The Animal Kingdom	18
The Bird World	24

CHAPTER TWO:

Taman Negara National Park and Surrounds	26

CHAPTER THREE:

Endau Rompin National Park	40

CHAPTER FOUR:

Royal Belum State Park and Temengor Forest Reserve	50

CHAPTER FIVE:

Bako, Kubah and Gunung Gading National Parks	58

CHAPTER SIX:

Gunung Mulu National Park and Niah National Park	76

CHAPTER SEVEN:
Batang Ai National Park and Lanjak Entimau
   Wildlife Sanctuary   90

CHAPTER EIGHT:
Danum Valley Conservation Area, Maliau Basin and
   Tabin Wildlife Reserve   102

CHAPTER NINE:
Kinabatangan Wildlife Sanctuary and Sepilok Orang-utan
   Rehabilitation Centre   118

CHAPTER TEN:
Kinabalu National Park   128

CHAPTER ELEVEN:
Sipadan Island and Pulau Tiga National Park   136

CHAPTER TWELVE:
Other Malaysian National Parks   142
Travel Tips   148
Selected Animal and Bird Gallery   150
Check List   156

INDEX   158

INTRODUCTION

THAILAND

Kota
Kinabalu
Sabah
MALAYSIA
KUALA   Sarawak
LUMPUR
SINGAPORE Kuching

INDONESIA

Malaysia is a country of contrasts and diversity where tradition and modernity are woven in a living tapestry of many colours, cultures and customs. Blessed with year-round sunshine, the land is endowed with stunning natural beauty: lofty mountains, mangrove forests, meandering rivers, golden beaches, paradise islands with pristine dive sites and one of the most diverse primordial rainforests in the world.

From ancient times, travellers and explorers have landed on the shores of Malaysia in search of adventure and riches. Today, Malaysia's green beauty forms the backdrop to challenging and exciting adventures not only for budding naturalists and die-hard jungle trekkers but also for families visiting for the first time.

Top Spots to See Birds

Taman Negara, Pahang
Endau Rompin National Park
Fraser's Hill, Pahang
Kinabalu National Park, Sabah
Danum Valley, Sabah
Bako National Park, Sarawak
Gunung Mulu National Park,
   Sarawak

Opposite, top to bottom: The picturesque shoreline of Pulau Tioman is renowned for its beautiful beach and great diving sites; the mangrove forest at low tide at Bako National Park often showcases fiddler crabs, mudskippers and monitor lizards; villages of Orang Asli in the Cameron Highlands offer a close encounter with the friendly tribes who welcome visitors to their settlements.

Introduction

Top Sites for Jungle Safari and Nature Adventures

Endau Rompin (Johor) – Lowland Rainforest

Taman Negara (Pahang) – Lowland Rainforest

Royal Belum National Park (Perak) – Hill Rainforest

Pangkor Laut Island (Perak) – Hill Rainforest

Pulau Langkawi (Kedah) – Mangrove and mixed forest

Danum Valley (Sabah) – Highland and Mountain Forest

Tabin Wildlife Reserve (Sabah) – Lowland Rainforest

Kinabalu National Park (Sabah) – Highland and Mountain Forest

Kinabatangan River (Sabah) – Freshwater swamp forest

Maliau Basin (Sabah) – Hill Forest

Sipadan Island (Sabah) – Coastal Forest and marine life

Bako National Park (Sarawak) – Mangrove and mixed forest

Gunung Mulu National Park (Sarawak) – Hill rainforest and limestone pinnacles

Batang Ai National Park (Sarawak) – Hill rainforest

PLANNING YOUR TRIP

It is prudent to plan your trip, taking into consideration fitness level required and time of the year. Most safaris are 'soft' adventures while others require stamina to endure long arduous trails deep into the jungle or hiking through mountainous terrain. When planning a trip, it is important to contact the relevant authority for advice as some places require bookings and permits. A network of well-planned air, road and river transport ensures easy year-round access to these enchanting places, with minimum threat to the environment, enabling visitors to observe the animal kingdom in its natural splendour. Accommodation in national parks varies from fairly simple chalets to comfortable lodges with basic amenities, while others have relatively luxurious hot showers and air conditioning. In some areas in Sarawak and Sabah, accommodation in traditional longhouses is available for visitors, where of course one should observe local customs and etiquette and respect the host's privacy. Most island resorts offer high standards of accommodation and luxury hotels with all the trimmings. These include the islands of Pangkor Laut, Langkawi, Tioman and Redang.

When visiting national parks or wildlife reserves, be scrupulous about no littering, no removal of plants or wildlife and generally respecting the environment. All national parks display their rules and regulations on a wooden bill board at the entrance to the parks, and many will advise: 'take only photographs and leave only footprints', which says it all.

The Essential Survival Kit

Before embarking on a jungle safari or a visit to a wildlife park, it would be wise to pack an essential survival kit and wear suitable attire. With such high humidity all year round and given the wilderness, light clothing made of natural fibre is best, which at the same time will give you protection against thorns, sharp leaves, insects and leeches (see panel, page 39). Cotton footless socks to be worn over your socks are available in some national park shops and travel clothing shops to prevent leech bites. Footwear should be hardy enough to withstand the rough terrain without slipping or ripping, and preferably waterproof or made of material that dries easily. Unless you are mountain climbing,

Planning your trip

heavy-duty boots are seldom necessary. Pack a plastic poncho to keep dry when it rains and insect repellent to ward off mosquitoes and other insects (it is also useful for repelling leeches). Pack a small medical kit of plasters and antiseptic cream in case of cuts and scratches from rocks or plants. To prevent dehydration, make sure you carry a supply of bottled water when out on a hike. Camera equipment should be stored in plastic bags for protection when it rains.

Generally speaking, there is more danger in a city than in the jungle. Although the forest is teeming with wildlife, visitors are seldom in any danger of encountering dangerous creatures. Large mammals, snakes and other dangerous animals are more likely to avoid human contact. On the other hand, due care should be exercised not to disturb them in their environment. Animals seldom attack unless provoked or threatened. Even snakes are rarely seen in the forest as they are well camouflaged as twigs or leaves. Another important rule to observe in the jungle is to avoid eating any plants or fruits that you are not familiar with. Some plants can sting or produce a nasty rash as a defence mechanism, so it is best not to disturb the natural vegetation. Always seek medical advice before embarking on a trip to make sure the right vaccination is used and proper medical precautions are observed. Visitors can sometimes get disorientated in dense forest so it advisable to travel in small groups or take a guide with you in case you get lost or injured. Wherever possible, try to

Peninsular Malaysia

Gulf of Thailand

Thailand — Songkhla — Hat Yai — Narathiwat — Langkawi — Alor Star — Ban Nang Sata — Kota Bharu — ANDAMAN SEA — Georgetown — Kuala Terengganu — Taiping — CAMERON HIGHLANDS — Gunung Tahan 2187m — Taman Negara National Park — Ipoh — Peninsular Malaysia — P. Pangkor — Lumut — Teluk Intan — Kuantan — KUALA LUMPUR — Klang — KLIA — Straits of Malacca — Endau Rompin National Park — P. Tioman — Mersing — Melaka — Sumatra — Pontian — Johor Bahru — P. Bengkalis — Kechil — P. Padang — P. Ramsang — Singapore — P. Rantua — Tanjungpinang

100 km
50 miles

Introduction

Nature Adventure Tips

• 'Take Only Pictures, Leave Only Footprints'
• Be prepared.
• Research your choice of trails and treks. Allow enough time to complete the entire route before darkness falls. Avoid straying off marked trails in pursuit of animals, unless accompanied by a guide.
• Assess your level of fitness and physical limits required for the journey.
• Always inform park officials or let someone know of your plans and destinations for the day, especially if you are venturing out alone.
• Pack adequate supplies of water and snacks to keep your energy level up. Unless trekking with a guide, avoid eating jungle fruits or drinking from wilderness water sources.
• An early dawn start gives you a better opportunity to sight animals and birds seeking food and the warmth of the early morning sun.
• Silent observation is advisable to avoid scaring off animals.

avoid exploring the forest on your own. If you do venture out alone, inform park officials or staff at your accommodation where you are going and do not wander off the main trails.

THE COUNTRY

Peninsular Malaysia (or West Malaysia) borders Thailand in the far north, petering out like an emerald finger to Singapore on the southern tip, while some 600km (375 miles) across the South China Sea lie Sabah and Sarawak (or East Malaysia) in the northern region of the island of Borneo. Malaysia is made up of thirteen states: the northern states of Perlis, Perak, Kedah and Penang; the southern states of Negri Sembilan, Melaka, Selangor and Johor; the east-coast states of Kelantan, Terengganu and Pahang plus the Federal Territory of Kuala Lumpur; and in East Malaysia the states of Sarawak and Sabah plus the Federal Territory of Labuan Island (off northern Borneo). The country covers a total area of 330,434km^2 (127,548 sq miles) of which 124,967km^2 (48,237 sq miles) covers Sarawak, the largest state of the country.

Malaysia's capital city, Kuala Lumpur, is a vibrant city that embraces modern progress without compromising its historical and cultural heritage. It serves as a gateway to the country and a major hub for international flights, serving between 15 and 25 million passengers a year. In line with Malaysia's eco-tourism principle, the state-of-the-art airport is designed to meet the 'airport in the forest and forest in the airport' concept. Small pockets of greenery are conserved within the airport, while the design of the airport itself is based on an abstract interpretation of the rainforest, with sweeping wooden structures representing spreading canopies.

Peninsular Malaysia has a well-developed infrastructure with railways and highways serving the country from north to south. The domestic flights network covers the whole county, with convenient connections even to remote rural areas in Sarawak and Sabah.

The Enchanting Forest

Straddling the equator, Malaysia's equatorial climate is blessed with perpetual sunshine and ample rainfall to nurture an

The Country

extravagantly verdant rainforest that has one of the highest biodiversities in the world. More than half of the country's land area is cloaked in evergreen forest with a bewildering variety of flora and fauna of breathtaking beauty. Malaysia is awash with nature's palette: emerald green of the jungles, ochre of the earth, granite grey of the mountain ranges and azure blue of the sea.

A walk in the rainforest is a mesmerizing experience. The forest is alive with melodic birdsong, the knocks of a woodpecker, the maniacal chatter of monkeys, the whooping calls of the gibbons and the grunting of wild boars, with a background jungle orchestra of hundreds of cicadas and crickets. You may catch a glimpse of an orang-utan, the flash of a flying squirrel, the graceful slither of a snake, elephants feasting on young shoots – all creatures shy, beautiful, great and small. Butterflies with ethereal wings of rainbow colours, giant golden spiders guarding their elaborate silky webs, moths (some the size of saucers) with divine works of art on their wings, and at night thousands of fireflies twinkling in their mangrove swamps like perpetual Christmas trees – these all make up an untouched Garden of Eden.

Types of Forest

Malaysia has the perfect climate for a luxuriant plant world. There are some 8500 species of vascular plants in Peninsular Malaysia and about 15,000 in Borneo, many of which occur in Sarawak and Sabah. The conditions in the humid forests are conducive to the growth of spores and germination of seeds. The jungle is dense with trees of varying sizes and heights, usually festooned with lianas and epiphytes (plants such as orchids that grow on other plants), strangler fig plants, palms and herbaceous plants. The forest is not normally a colourful place awash with fruit-laden trees and flowers in bloom, but it has a very complex and amazing ecological system that supports a wildlife population. In the mountainous region, condensation from the lowlands shrouds the jungles with fine mist and is breathtakingly beautiful in the early morning.

The Malaysian rainforests can be divided into three distinct types: lowland and hill rainforest, montane or mountain forest and coastal mangrove. There are two categories of forest, namely

More Nature Adventure Tips

• Wear comfortable attire: loose long-sleeved cotton tops and long trousers to prevent insects and leech bites and scratches from thorny plants. Choose sturdy non-slip shoes with ankle support and good traction that can endure rough terrain and wet jungle floors. Wear leech socks or long socks to prevent leeches getting into your shoes.

• Carry a plastic poncho for rainwear and plastic bags for camera equipment.

• Wear a hat to shade your head from the tropical sun, and apply an ecologically friendly insect repellent.

• Obey park rules and regulations.

• Summon your spirit of adventure to enjoy the magic of the rainforest.

Introduction

primary and secondary. Primary forest is virgin forest untouched by humans, while secondary forests are jungles that have been logged over or are selectively cut for commercial purposes.

Coastal Forest

Sandwiched between the sea and fresh water are the mangrove forests, sprouting from sandy mud and brackish water. Their protruding exposed roots can tolerate the salinity and lack of aeration caused by the inundation of tidal sea water. Mangroves are productive trees that fruit continuously. They support a diverse array of wildlife such as crab-eating macaques, water monitor lizards, mud skippers, crabs, snakes, water birds and even sea eagles. Mangrove forests are best explored in small boats that weave among the banks and streams of this swampy forest and its fascinating wild world. Mangrove plants produce litter (leaves, twigs, fruits and flowers) that is taken by crabs and broken down by fungi and bacteria to provide nutrients to other animals. These micro-organisms, loaded with protein, are then consumed by fish and prawns that produce waste used by

Types of Forest

crustaceans and molluscs, thus forming an ecological circle of life. Where there is a mangrove swamp, there is always a rich source of fish and prawns, the largest intact stretch being on the eastern coast of Sabah, famous for its seafood.

In areas where fresh water from inland sources frequently flows into the sea bringing nutrient silts, nipah palms (*Nypa fruticans*), or *Attap* in Malay, grow abundantly, fringing the banks in the lower reaches of the rivers. It is a versatile palm. The fronds are used for thatching roofs in coastal villages while the large flower buds produce sugar that is widely used in local desserts and cooking. Where there are no nipahs or mangrove, sandy beaches fringe most of the coastline. The vegetation here consists mainly of coconut palms and screw pine (*Pandanus spiralis*) – a large member of the pandan family with long pleated leaves barbed with prickles. The smaller species of pandan are commonly used in flavouring traditional cakes and sweets, while another species provides materials for local handicrafts such as mats, baskets and bags. Casuarina pine trees are another phenomenon on sandy beaches. They help reduce erosion and act as windbreakers.

Freshwater Swamp Forest

These are inland forests where there is inefficient drainage of fresh water, periodic flooding on alluvial soil, and peat soil formed from semi-decayed plant material. The alluvial swamp is mostly found in Sabah especially on the flood plain of the Kinabatangan River which offers one of the best river safaris in Malaysia. The fertile swamp forest yields an abundance of leafy fruiting trees particularly the strangler figs that provide food for so many birds and mammals. It supports a rich ecosystem of wildlife including proboscis monkeys, orang-utans, macaques, elephant, banteng and water birds.

Nature cleverly allows different trees to fruit at different times of the year, not following any particular season, hence there is constant supply of fruits all year round and therefore also abundant wildlife. Peat swamp is commonly found in Sarawak and some coastal regions of southern Peninsular Malaysia. It is highly infertile but produces valuable hardwoods which are prized for timber. Without the presence of fruiting trees, wildlife is poor

Some Bird Species Found In Peninsular Malaysia's Forests

Grey-headed Fishing Eagle
Crested Serpent Eagle
Crested Goshawk
Crested Fireback Pheasant
Great Argus Pheasant
Green-winged Pigeon
Plaintive Cuckoo
Greater Coucal
Dusky Eagle Owl
Cinnamon-rumped Trogon
Blue-banded Kingfisher
White-crowned Hornbill
Wreathed Hornbill
Rhinoceros Hornbill
Great Slaty Woodpecker
Black-and-Yellow Broadbill
Garnet Pitta
Common Green Magpie
Rail Babbler
White-rumped Shama
Rufous-tailed Tailorbird
Asian Paradise Flycatcher
Red-throated Sunbird
Orange-bellied Flowerpecker
Little Spiderhunter

Introduction

Some Mammals Found in Peninsular Malaysia's Forests

(Risk status given in brackets)
Tiger (Endangered)
Black flying squirrel
Binturong (Lower Risk)
Small-tooth palm civet (Lower Risk)
Asiatic brush-tailed porcupine (Lower Risk)
Seladang (Gaur) (Vulnerable)
Asiatic golden cat (Vulnerable)
Asian elephant (Endangered)
Malayan flying lemur
Sun bear
Short-tailed mongoose
White-handed gibbon (Lower Risk)
Smooth-coated otter (Vulnerable)
Long-tailed macaque (Lower Risk)
Pig-tailed macaque (Vulnerable)
Banded leaf monkey (Lower Risk)
Malayan pangolin (Lower Risk)
Clouded leopard (Vulnerable)
Marbled cat (Vulnerable)
Leopard cat
Greater mousedeer
Sambar
Bearded pig (Lower Risk)
Wild boar (Lower Risk)
Malayan tapir (Vulnerable)
Oriental small-clawed otter
Smooth-coated otter
Slow loris (Lower Risk)
Asian palm civet (Lower Risk)
Silvered leaf monkey

in this type of forest. The spongy soil of the peat swamp, however, helps to reduce flooding with its sponge-like propensity to absorb water.

Dipterocarp Forest

The dipterocarp forest is the dominant vegetation found in the mountainous and hilly region of the country at altitudes of up to 900m (2953ft). These large trees grow to great heights, supported by buttress roots that anchor themselves to the ground, and tower above smaller vegetation like a giant green umbrella. The dark scaly bark is usually encrusted with resin known as *damar* in Malay to resist infection by bacteria, fungi and insects. Before the advent of synthetic substitutes, *damar* used to be exported to Europe for the manufacture of paints, varnish and linoleum. In rural settlements in Malaysia, it is still used as fuel for lighting lamps and by fishermen to caulk leaky boats. The trees in this type of forest are slow-growing due to the density of the vegetation – only 2% of natural light ever reaches the ground.

The damp, humid conditions are the perfect breeding ground for insects and fungi, which the trees fight off by producing indigestible carbohydrate fibres or tannins that are foul-tasting or toxic. Of course some, like quinine, have medicinal value. Trees that have succumbed to invasion by insects or fungi are peppered with holes and provide homes for bats, porcupines, snakes, small mammals or hornbills.

Ironwood, known locally as *belian* (*Eusideroxylon zwageri*), is found in Sarawak and Sabah. Some of these hardwoods are thousands of years old; even after the death of the trees, the slow decay lasts for hundreds of years. Surprisingly there are few flowering and fruiting plants in this type of forest and the fruits grow in seasons mainly between July and September. Most dipterocarp forest fruits are inedible to humans, except one: the durian (*Durio*), known locally as 'King of the Fruit', of which there are 30 known species. These massive fruits have a thick, spiky green or yellow skin with creamy flesh encased round large seeds that are fragrant to lovers of these fruits, but to those uninitiated in the delights of these unique fruits, they can repulse as they have a strong, very unpleasant smell, hence the description: 'tastes like heaven and

Types of Forest

smells like hell.' Among other edible fruits growing wild here are mango (*Mangifera*), rambutan (*Nephelium*) and bread fruit (*Artocarpus*) – all supplying a rich buffet for mammals and birds.

The holy grail of the forest is the Rafflesia (*R. arnoldii*) found in the hill ranges of northern Peninsular Malaysia, Sarawak and Sabah, usually at altitudes of 500–700m (1640–2300ft) above sea level (*see* page 70). It is the largest flower in the world and can grow up to 1m (3.3ft) in diameter. It is a parasite without any leaves, stems or roots. In order to absorb nutrients, it grows on the root of the Tetrastigma (*Vitaceae*), a vine belonging to the grape family. The purple cabbage-like bud takes many months to flower to its full size of a five-petal structure. It has a short lifespan of five to seven days only, looks and smells like rotting meat and is known as 'corpse flower' in the local language. To see one in bloom is a very rare experience, but some forest reserves in Sabah, Sarawak and Peninsular Malaysia have a Rafflesia watch where visitors can get the latest information on when a flower is in bloom.

Below: Jackfruit (Artocarpus heterophyllus), *or* Buah Nangka *in Malay, is the largest tree-borne fruit in the world and can weigh up to 36kg (80lb). Its fragrant, chewy flesh is a favourite among Malaysians.*

Another exceptional plant is the tualang tree (*Koompassia excelsa*) that belongs to the legume family. It is commonly found in the low-altitude forest of Peninsular Malaysia and in Sarawak and Sabah. The tualang trees, though abundant in numbers, are always found in isolation and never in clusters over large areas. With its towering trunk clad in smooth whitish bark soaring up to 75m (246ft) tall, it is a majestic symbol. It is known as *tapang* in Sarawak and *mengaris* in Sabah. Due to its gigantic size and huge buttresses, it is rarely felled for timber and is usually spared in land cleared for agriculture. Local folk revere this tree as having spiritual significance, and it is the favourite hive choice of the Asian rock bees that provide honey for locals. It is not unusual to see dozens of parabolic

Introduction

Some Reptiles Found in Peninsular Malaysia's Forests

Common water monitor
Yellow-ringed cat snake
Banded krait
Common flying dragon
Reticulated python
Black marsh turtle (Vulnerable)
False gharial (Endangered)
Siamese crocodile (Critical)
Banded keelback
Malaysia giant turtle (Endangered)

honeycombs suspended from its tall branches. Its smooth bark prevents sunbears and other animals from reaching the hives but it does not prevent humans from harvesting the honeycombs.

Heath Forests

Land near sea level on flat terrains or ridges is often covered by heath forest where trees with small thick leaves are found scattered on infertile sandy stretches. The thick leaves are nature's way of preventing attack by insects and animals and therefore very little wildlife is found in heath forest. A notable feature of heath forest plants is their symbiotic relationship with ants that live in bulbous pods that adhere to the trees. In return for giving them a home, the ants protect the trees against marauding caterpillars that consume the leaves but at the same time provide nutrients to the plants with their waste. The heath forest is also an ideal locale for the carnivorous pitcher plants. There are many species but the most commonly found are the *Nepenthaceae* and *Sarraceniaceae* families. Their cup-shaped structures, laced with nectar, act like traps for insects that slip down the smooth sides of the cup and are digested by the plant.

Montane Forests

Between the lowland and mountain ranges are the montane forests, found at varying altitudes from 600–1200m (1970–3940ft) in Sabah. Due to the altitude, no dipterocarp and legume trees are found here. The main vegetation types are plants not usually associated with the tropics: oak trees (*Fagaceae*), myrtle (*Myrtaceae*) and laurel (*Lauraceae*) along with magnolias, rhododendrons and raspberries. Gnarled bushes and moss-covered trees dominate the forest and there are many species of orchids and other epiphytes and pitcher plants. The air is often misty and cold with poor visibility. Relatively few animals, insects and birds are found here.

River Deep, Mountain High

Malaysia is a natural wonder at its grandest scale, with ecosystems determined by rainfall, terrain, the contour of mountains and hills, the rivers, the geology, altitude, drainage and other environmental factors. It is a land of diverse topography and physical geography. The Banjaran Titiwangsa, or Main Range, forms the backbone of

River Deep, Mountain High

Peninsular Malaysia, separating the east and west coasts, the highest peak being Gunung Tahan standing at 2187m (7176ft) high in Pahang. In East Malaysia, Sabah boasts the highest mountain in Southeast Asia, Mount Kinabalu at 4101m (13,455ft) high in the Crocker Range. In Sarawak, Gunung Mulu harbours the largest natural cave systems in the world (the Mulu Caves), while its river, the Rajang, is the longest river in Malaysia at 563km (350 miles) long.

Offshore in the South China Sea, rugged islands surrounded by coral reefs and crystal clear blue water open up an underwater world of dazzling colour, with marine life of every description. The east coast of the Peninsula has sandy beaches stretching from Kelantan in the north to Johor in the south.

Due to its physical features and heavy rainfall, Malaysia has a large network of rivers across the country serving as arteries for transport, particularly in the rural areas. Rivers in rugged terrain provide thrilling white-water rafting for the adventurous. On the western coast of Peninsular Malaysia and in Sarawak and Sabah, alluvial coastal plains are fringed with mangroves and backed by a rugged mountainous interior.

Temperatures are high all year round, averaging 26°C (79°F) in the coastal region while the hill resorts such as Cameron Highlands have a mean temperature of 18°C (64°F). The average relative humidity is 80%. The northeast monsoon blows across the South China Sea from October to March bringing heavy rain to the east coasts of the Peninsula, and Sarawak and Sabah.

Roughly half of the rainforest has been cleared for development, urbanization, deforestation and agriculture. Malaysia, however, has a progressive policy of eco-tourism to conserve its national heritage. Large tracts of rainforest throughout the country have been declared protective forest reserves and national parks, thus ensuring that the wildlife and their habitats are protected for tourism and for future generations. The country's diverse ecosystems offer a wide variety of wildlife adventures: river and jungle safaris, wildlife observation from constructed hides, jungle treks, camping, animal sanctuaries, such as the renowned Sepilok

Some Bird Species Found in Malaysian Borneo

Wrinkled Hornbill (Near Threatened)
Rhinoceros Hornbill (Near Threatened)
Yellow-Bellied Bulbul
Red-Throated Pipit
Spectacled Spiderhunter
Great Egret
Purple Heron
Oriental Darter (Near Threatened)
Little Ringed Plover
Lesser Green Leaf Bird (Near Threatened)
Violet Cuckoo
Pied Harrier
White Crown Shama
Dusky Broadbill
Blue-breasted Quail
Grey-headed Canary Flycatcher
Black and Red Broadbill
Grey-capped Woodpecker
Scarlet-backed Flowerpecker
Hair-crested Drongo
Blue-crowned Hanging Parrot
Ruddy Kingfisher
Peregrine Falcon
Hill Myna
Bornean Barbet

Introduction

The Big Six

Top of the endangered species found in the Malaysian forests are elephants, big cats (tiger, leopard and clouded leopard), rhinoceros, tapir, wild cattle (*seladang* and *banteng*) and orang-utan. They are rare and to spot them in the wild is quite a thrill.

Orang-utan Rehabilitation Centre in Sabah, and the natural wonder of Mulu Caves in Sarawak.

Malaysia is one of the twelve most biologically diverse countries in the world. There are over 600 species of birds found in Peninsular Malaysia and about 580 species in Malaysian Borneo, of which nearly two-thirds are indigenous; 216 species of mammals are known in Peninsular Malaysia, and 218 in Sabah and Sarawak, of which 40 species found in the latter are endemic to Borneo. The flora ecosystem is equally rich, with 1200 species of orchids found in Mount Kinabalu, for example, and more than 1160 species of ferns throughout the country.

The Animal Kingdom

Going Wild on Pangkor Laut Island

The privately owned island of Pangkor Laut in Perak is a hidden jewel of nature's bounty. A tiny island of just over 120 hectares (298 acres), it is an ultra-luxury resort with an eco mantra. The villas are sympathetically built to blend with nature, conserving as much as possible the ancient coastal hill forest and its denizens. The island abounds with exotic flora, including rare orchids and trees. The most commonly spotted fauna are macaques, sea otters, monitor lizards, bats and pangolins, while the avian inhabitants include the Indian Peacock, Oriental Pied Hornbill, eagles, Malaysian Plover, herons, woodpeckers, bulbuls, owls and kingfishers. The late Pavarotti declared this island a 'paradise'.

The verdant forests of Malaysia host a wide variety of animals and plants. While there may be a great variety of species, the number of individual animals is relatively small and there are no large herds of animals as on the African plains for example. The only animals living in fairly large herds are elephants, which are found in Peninsular Malaysia and Sabah. Due to the hot and humid climate and by a natural selection of evolution, large animals like

The Animal Kingdom

elephants, tigers, leopards, clouded leopards, rhinos, bears, tapirs and the like are rare in the tropical forest. The damp and warm environment in the jungle harbours parasites and diseases that keep their number in check and some rainforest plants have a defence mechanism of producing toxic and indigestible chemicals to prevent mammals from eating them. Herbivores like deer, wild cattle and elephants survive on large quantities of grass and succulent plants and the shortage of their diet is a factor explaining their small numbers in the forest. Although the forests reverberate with the sound of animals and birds, the dense vegetation does not make it easy to spot animals in the wild unlike, once again, the open savannah plains of Africa. But the rare sightings amid the wondrous trees and plants make a safari in the rainforest intriguing and rewarding. It needs patience and clever detective work by forest rangers or guides to look for tell-tale signs such as pug marks and animal droppings to establish the type of animals present in the area. Deer, wild boars and particularly the chattering monkeys are most commonly sighted in the wild.

Elephants

The endangered Asian elephants in Malaysia are the largest mammals found in the forest but, owing to loss of habitat through urbanization and agriculture, the herds are dwindling in numbers and are scattered in various forest reserves and parks. The Asian elephants in Malaysia are smaller than their Indian cousins and much smaller than African elephants. In Sabah, the Borneo pygmy elephants are the smallest species of elephant in the world. Encountering elephants in the wild is a matter of luck and in Peninsular Malaysia they are found mostly around the Taman Negara area and in Endau Rompin National Park. In Sabah, herds of elephants are often seen in Danum Valley and along the Kinabatangan River, especially during the dry season when the elephants come out of the forest to drink and swim in the river.

Wild Cattle (*Seladang* and *Banteng*)

Wild cattle such as the *seladang* and *banteng* are the second largest mammals found in Malaysia and both are more powerfully built than domestic cattle. The *seladang* is a magnificent beast with a Herculean muscular body, dark tan hide and white stocking-like

Some Mammals Found in Malaysian Borneo

Binturong (Lower Risk)
Prevost squirrel
Bay cat (Endangered)
Otter civet (Endangered)
Asian elephant (Endangered)
Orang-utan (Endangered)
Proboscis monkey (Endangered)
Clouded leopard (Vulnerable)
Sumatran rhinoceros (Critical)
Bornean mountain ground squirrel
Tufted pygmy squirrel (Lower Risk)
Sun bear
Collared mongoose (Lower Risk)
Bornean gibbon (Lower Risk)
Thick-spined porcupine
Long-tailed macaque (Lower Risk)
Slow loris (Lower Risk)
Marbled cat (Vulnerable)
Red leaf monkey (Lower Risk)
Western tarsier
Sambar
Lesser mousedeer
Long-tailed porcupine
Bearded pig

Opposite: An infant dusky leaf monkey strikes a pretty pose; its distinctive spectacled marking gives the species its nickname of spectacled langur.

Introduction

**Some Reptiles Found
in Malaysian Borneo**

Oriental whipsnake
Marble cat snake
Red-headed krait
Striped bridal snake
King cobra
Borneo forest dragon
Rough neck monitor
Painted terrapin (Critical)
Estuarine crocodile (Lower Risk)
Asian leaf turtle

markings on its legs. These rare and shy creatures live in habitats near Taman Negara and forested areas in Pahang and Kelantan, but are seldom spotted. The *banteng* are just as rare and have occasionally been sighted in the lowland areas of eastern Sabah. Both species visit natural mineral sources and graze on grasslands cleared by people for planting rice.

Rhinoceros

Malaysia is also home to the smallest rhinoceros in the world. Usually referred to as the Sumatran or Asian Two-horned rhinoceros or even hairy rhinos, these animals are so rare that at one time they were feared to be extinct. The government has started a programme to capture rhinos in unprotected areas and to hold them in captivity in the hope of establishing a breeding programme. Sadly, the horns of the rhinos carry a death sentence for the species as they are hunted for use in Chinese medicine. Despite the fact that there is no scientific proof at all that rhino horns have any medicinal value, their demand from traditional Chinese herbalists has not decreased. The hairy rhino is a solitary animal though groups of two or three, possibly a family unit, have been seen. The tell-tale sign of the presence of a rhino is found in mud wallows that have been dug and marked by its distinctive footprint of three large toenails on each foot, one in front and one on each side. Rhinos can be found in the Endau Rompin area and in Tabin Wildlife Reserve and Danum Valley in Sabah, albeit rarely.

Tapirs

Another fascinating and rare creature is the Malay tapir. Related to the rhinoceros family, it is smaller than a rhino but larger than a wild pig. It has smooth, black and white markings on its body with a long head tapering into a flexible mini-trunk. Tapirs are found in and around Taman Negara and have even been spotted near forested areas in Kuala Lumpur. They are more common than the rhinoceros.

Big Cats (Tiger, Leopard and Clouded Leopard)

Tigers, leopards and clouded leopards are highly endangered and to see one in the wild is like striking gold. As their natural habitat has shrunk through deforestation for logging and plantations,

The Animal Kingdom

these big cats have been spotted in oil palm and fruit plantations and the conflicts between humans and animals sometimes end up in tragedy on both sides. They are very secretive animals and the dense forest provides an excellent camouflage for them. They are found mostly in Taman Negara and Endau Rompin national parks area. Although there are no tigers in Sabah and Sarawak, leopards and clouded leopards are found deep in the jungle of these two Bornean states. In March 2007, scientists discovered that the clouded leopard in Borneo is an entirely new species of cat from its west Malaysian cousins. The Bornean clouded leopard has small cloud markings, greyer fur and double dorsal stripes while the west Malaysian clouded leopard has large cloud marking with fewer spots within the cloud markings. The big cats are magnificent creatures of great beauty.

Their much smaller cousin, the leopard cat, is the size of a domestic cat. With its beautiful marking of honey-coloured fur peppered with black spots, they are sometimes seen along remote tracks near a plantation. The leopard cat looks like a miniature leopard but meows like a domestic cat.

Below: The Sumatran rhino, the smallest rhinoceros in the world, is highly endangered and is rarely seen in the wild as its numbers have dwindled drastically due to loss of habitat and poaching.

Introduction

Bornean Bearded Pig

The bearded pig *(Sus barbatus)* is a ubiquitous denizen of the Malaysian jungle, particularly in mangrove and secondary forest. With beady eyes, pointed ears, a long head covered with bristly beard and a prominent snout, it has a face that only its mother would call beautiful. Its powerful torso is covered in reddish-brown or greyish-white hair. Its favourite hangouts are mud wallows, salt licks and around palm oil plantations where it can pilfer the young shoots of palms. It feeds on roots, shoots, herbs, earthworms, seedlings and fruits. It tends to follow the macaques or gibbons to a fruit tree, waiting for a windfall of fruits discarded by the primates. Bearded pigs live in family groups, usually a mother and her piglets who will remain with her for roughly a year. They migrate yearly in large herds of up to 100 or more and move at night on well-trodden paths; they have been seen crossing rivers and mountain ranges. Their main predators are tiger, leopard, clouded leopard and pythons.

Orang-utan

There are many species of monkeys and apes in both east and west Malaysia but the most appealing and intelligent is the orang-utan or 'Man of the forest'. A walk through the rainforest may reveal many of their empty nests high up in the canopy but to spot one in the wild is very rare. They are found only in Sabah and Sarawak. With their natural habitat shrinking fast, they are high on the endangered list and rehabilitation centres have been set up in Sepilok in Sabah and at Semonggok in Sawarak to house confiscated pets or displaced or injured orang-utans found in the wild. During the wild fig fruiting season at the end of the year, wild orang-utans are sometimes seen along the Kinabatangan River in Sabah. Their bright orange fur and human-like behaviour are a fascinating sight.

Pigs, Monkeys and Langurs

Bearded pigs and common wild pigs are often found rooting for food near the edge of the forest and are not adverse to hanging around accommodations in national parks or using their porcine

The Animal Kingdom

charm to appeal to visitors for a handout – a practice highly discouraged by the park authorities.

Primates are commonly encountered in the forest, coastal areas and around villages. The most conspicuous and nosiest are the long-tailed and pig-tailed macaque monkeys. They move in big groups and often make a nuisance of themselves in plantations, park chalets and resorts but provide a source of amusement to visitors with their antics and mischief. They are highly intelligent and are skilled in breaking into chalets and hotels, helping themselves to the contents of the minibars and trashing the rooms like naughty children.

However cute they may seem, they are wild animals and should never be fed, approached or encouraged. It is always advisable to lock all doors and windows when leaving the room unless you want to come back to a room ravaged by monkey tricks. The leaf monkeys or langurs are more shy and do not have the rowdy reputation of the macaques. There are seven species of langurs in Malaysia and they are more attractive than the macaques, especially the dusky leaf monkey or spectacled langur because of its sooty coloured coat and white-rimmed eyes. The red leaf monkey is similar in colour to the orang-utan and has been confused with the ape. The difference between an ape and a monkey is that monkeys have tails while apes do not. The most spectacular monkeys are the proboscis monkeys found only in the coastal forests of Sabah and Sarawak. They have reddish and white fur and are active in the early morning and late afternoon. The male is massive, weighing over 20kg (44lb), and is endowed with a pendulous nose and rotund belly. Other commonly sighted creatures are deer and mousedeer, often solitary rather than in

Above: A male proboscis monkey, with its huge, pendulous nose and large paunch, keeps a watchful eye on his harem and young while feasting on the leaves of mangrove trees.

Opposite: Bearded pigs, so called because of the bristly whiskers on their long snouts, are commonly found in the Malaysian forests and along river banks foraging for food.

Introduction

herds. Arboreal creatures like the slow-moving slow loris and tarsiers are often spotted on night safari when they are most active. The tarsier is one of the strangest mammals in the forests and is found only in Sarawak and Sabah. It is a tiny creature, about 13cm (5in) long excluding its tail, has enormous eyes and possesses frog-like hands and feet. The slow loris is a rather tubby primate with soft fur and short tail and, although slow by name, is not as slow to bolt when frightened.

Below: The majestic White-bellied Sea Eagle perches on a branch, ready to swoop down on its unsuspecting prey – usually fish.

The Bird World

The luxuriant rainforest, which harbours millions of insects and vast numbers of fruiting trees, is the ideal habitat for birds that come in a bewildering array of colours and sizes – an ornithologist's paradise. An experienced bird-watcher can identify, from sight and sound, as many as sixty birds on a day's outing in the lowland dipterocarp forest. Birds are more easily seen than mammals. The country's location on the Australasian cross-migratory paths also makes it a host to over 200 migratory birds.

A sure way to spot birds of various species and colours is to lie quietly in wait, perhaps near a fruiting tree, especially the strangler fig trees which are recognizable by their tangle of gnarled roots and red and yellow fruits. The strangler fig tree starts life by attaching itself to a host tree, eventually killing

The Bird World

it when capable of surviving on its own. Some stranglers may grow up to 50m (164ft) tall. The fruits are food favourites for hornbills, barbets, pigeons, Green Magpies and many other bird species, all competing with mammals and primates. The hornbills are easy to spot due to their large size, squawking calls and noisy wing-beats in flight.

Birds are also abundantly found in secluded valleys in the depths of the dipterocarp forest. An experienced ornithologist can identify a species from bird calls. Sometimes a bird will advance if you can imitate its call. Some birds can easily be spotted by following the direction of the calls. The Garnet Pitta has a low-pitched monotonous whistle. It is a ground-dwelling bird preferring damp surroundings where it feeds on insects, grubs and snails. The attractive Green Broadbill sings sweetly in the low canopy while pheasants and partridges are often seen foraging for fallen fruits and insects. Flashes of red and black among the green canopy will probably belong to a species of trogon or the minivets. Raptors such as sparrowhawks and eagles are seen perched high on branches seeking prey, their whereabouts betrayed by piercing calls that send small mammals scampering for cover. The hooting of owls is the night song of the forest. They are regularly seen on night safaris.

Along the rivers, a variety of kingfishers such as the Common Kingfisher, Blue-banded Kingfisher, Stock-billed and others can be seen darting in and out of the water feeding on fish. White Egrets, herons, storks and Oriental Darters are found along river banks. A wide range of birds can be found almost everywhere in Malaysia year round, the species determined by the ecological zones in the forests or other terrain.

Tips for Twitchers

- Do research on sites and bird species likely to be found.
- Take a pair of good binoculars to locate and identify birds at a distance and in flight.
- The best time to watch birds is early morning and late afternoon when the temperature is cooler.
- Most birds have regular feeding habits and patterns. Mudflats at low tide and around fruiting trees are good locations.

Below: The White-throated Kingfisher is commonly found throughout Malaysia.

TAMAN NEGARA NATIONAL PARK AND SURROUNDS

Taman Negara is the first national park and largest conservation area in Malaysia and one of the oldest primeval rainforests in the world dating back 130 million years. Legislated as a national park in 1938–39, Taman Negara was originally called King George V National Park but renamed Taman Negara (which simply means national park in Malay) after the nation's independence in 1957. It was gazetted as a forest conservation project with a mission statement to 'utilise the land within the park in perpetuity for propagation, protection and preservation of indigenous flora and fauna'.

Top Ten

Fireback Pheasant
Hornbills
Blue-throated Bee-eater
Garnet Pitta
Straw-headed Bulbul
Siamang
Tiger
Leopard
Asian elephant
Sumatran rhinoceros

Opposite top: *Thick foliage along the Sungai Tembeling provides a natural habitat for birds and snakes.*
Opposite centre: *A wooden park boat carries visitors to the park headquarters at Kuala Tahan on Sungai Tembeling.*
Opposite bottom: *Lush forest framing the Kuala Sungai Tahan completes the landscape of beautiful riverine scenery.*

Taman Negara National Park and Surrounds

Taman Negara

Taman Negara National Park

Location: 260km (162 miles) from Kuala Lumpur.
Size: 4343km² (1676 sq miles).
Altitude: 300–2187m (984–7176ft).
Of interest: Camping, fishing, trekking, bird-watching, shooting the rapids, wildlife observation from jungle hides, and nature walks.

Taman Negara National Park covers an area of 4343km² (1676 sq miles) of pristine virgin forest in undulating terrain at altitudes ranging from less than 300m (984ft) to the summit of Gunung Tahan, the tallest mountain in Peninsular Malaysia, at 2187m (7176ft). It dominates the central highland core of the mighty Titiwangsa Mountain Range that forms the backbone of Peninsular Malaysia. Taman Negara spans three states: the biggest area, in Pahang, occupies 2477km² (956 sq miles), followed by Kelantan in the north with 1043km² (403 sq miles) and Terengganu on the east coast with 853km² (329 sq miles). Its vegetation ranges from lowland and hill dipterocarp forests and riverine vegetation, through to oaks and laurel at the mid-altitude, up to the dwarf upper montane ericaceous foliage of the summit of Gunung Tahan. It is the best protected forest in Malaysia and considered to be one of the greatest natural wonders of the world, with its flora and fauna undisturbed for millions of years. It is a paradise for caring nature lovers, adventure-seekers and environmentalists.

Below: Sambar deer foraging in the forest are often spotted on night safari in the jungle, with their red eyes glowing in the dark.

Flora and Fauna

As Malaysia's premier national park and thanks to its pristine ecosystem, Taman Negara has one of the richest biodiversities in the world. There are 200 species of plants per hectare, including some of the region's rarest orchids and ferns. There are also

Flora and Fauna

reportedly 200 species of animals such as the guar or *seladang*, sambar deer, wild pigs, tapir, Asian elephants, Malayan tigers, leopard, sun bear and Sumatran rhinoceros. The sun bear is the only species of bear found in Malaysia. It is also known as the honey bear as it spends most of its time raiding beehives. The highly endangered Sumatran rhinoceros is one of the rarest mammals in Taman Negara. Sighting of large mammals is very rare due to the density of the vegetation, their shy nature and their ability to camouflage themselves. They are more likely to be heard than seen, though the tell-tale signs of disturbed vegetation, footprints and droppings are indications of their presence. The most commonly sighted and raucous animals in the forest are the macaques, leaf monkeys, white-handed gibbons and the larger black *siamang* gibbons. The white-handed gibbons got their names, of course, from their white gloves even though their fur ranges from beige to black. The gibbons have a very distinctive 'wak wak' whooping call, hence they are known locally as '*wak wak*'.

There are over 600 species of birds in Peninsular Malaysia of which 380 species have been recorded in the park. Pheasants are of particular interest, with two Fireback Pheasants, the Malayan Peacock and Mountain Peacock pheasants, together with the Great Argus and Crested Argus. The most commonly seen lowland birds are the hornbills, the beautiful Green Broadbill, Grey-headed Fish Eagle, kingfishers, drongos and Blue-throated Bee-eaters. Others include the Garnet Pitta, with its striking red belly, while Yellow-crowned Barbets are more usually heard than seen, except at fruiting seasons when they congregate in large numbers at strangler fig trees which also attract the Thick-billed Pigeons, distinguished by their guttural gurgles. The warm humid forests are ideal homes for insects, reptiles and amphibians of which there are more than 100 species of snakes, frogs, crocodiles, lizards, turtles and tortoises – all ancient animal species that walked the earth 300 million years ago. Over 1000 species of butterflies are found here, dazzling the forest with their colourful ethereal wings. Distinctive butterfly species include the beautiful Smaller Wood Nymph; the handsome and widespread Great Egg-fly; The Red Helen with its beautifully marked swallowtail wings; the strikingly huge Common Birdwing, and the magnificent Rajah Brooke's Birdwing with a wingspan of up to 18cm (7in), named by the discoverer Alfred Russel Wallace in honour of Sir James Brooke, the first White Rajah of Sarawak.

Park Authority Information and Advice

1. Visitors can get lost in Taman Negara, usually when they stray from the marked trails. Thus, visitors are advised to take a guide.

2. Flash floods can occur in rivers like Sungai Tahan. Do not leave your belongings by the water's edge, and when swimming be alert to sudden mud slides at the water. Never camp too close to the water.

3. From time to time, large trees fall in the forest or branches drop. Strong winds are rare, and usually of short duration. If you are in the forest during a storm, sit it out under a gap in the canopy.

4. Among the hardest animals to find in the rain forest are snakes, but people lucky enough to see them usually admire them from a distance. There is no record of a park visitor ever being bitten by a poisonous snake, and most Malaysian species pose no threat to human life.

5. Wasp stings hurt for a short while only, but hornet stings can be very painful for hours. If you are allergic to stings, always carry suitable medication.

6. No Taman Negara visitors have as yet been eaten by tigers, trampled by raging bull elephants, or mauled by bears. If you happen to see any of these animals, stay calm and don't panic. The animal will usually move away.

Taman Negara National Park and Surrounds

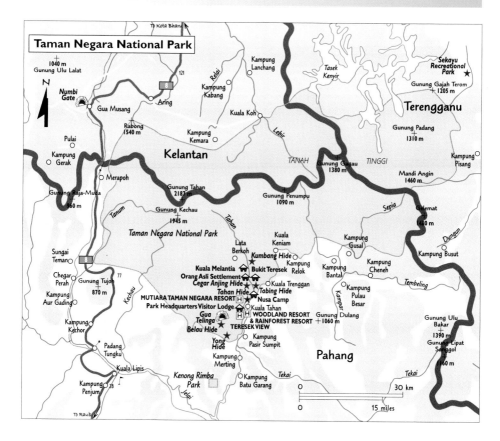

Epiphytes such as orchids and ferns grow in abundance in Taman Negara, especially along the banks of two of the rivers – Sungai Tahan and Sungai Keniam – while palm flora thrive well in the higher montane forest in the Tahan massif, the only known home of the *Livistona tahanensis*, a graceful small fan-palm endemic to this region.

Taman Negara National Park offers a variety of wilderness activities to suit all levels of fitness and interest: there are leisure nature walks, interpretive trails with descriptions of the flora and fauna, more challenging jungle trekking, animal observation from hides, river safaris and night safaris, and even adrenaline-pumping activities like shooting the rapids and sky-walking on the lofty forest canopy.

Wildlife Watch in Jungle Hides

Wildlife Watch In Jungle Hides

Wildlife watching requires the patience of a saint and the enthusiasm of a child on a visit to a sweet shop. Nature did not intend its creations to be a spectator sport and its creatures do not perform to command. It is a matter of chance and luck and when you do have successful sightings of a mammal, bird or reptile, it is a privilege, a moment to treasure.

An excellent way to observe wildlife in Taman Negara is to wait in jungle hides at night. There are six hides scattered around the park which can be reached on foot or by boat. Overnight stays in some hides can be arranged. Kumbang Hide is a 40-minute boat ride from the park headquarters at Kuala Tahan followed by an additional 45-minute walk to the hide, or a 5-hour trek over 11km (7 miles). Cegar Anjing Hide is 2.9km (1.8 miles) from the headquarters; Yong Hide is 3.9km (2.4 miles) away, a 2-hour walk or a 20-minute boat ride plus a 10-minute walk. But the most popular is Tahan Hide which is just a 5-minute walk from the headquarters. The other two hides are Belau Hide, 3km (1.8 miles) and a 1.5-hour walk or 15 minutes by boat, and Tabing Hide, 3.1km (1.9 miles) away, an hour's trek or a boat ride with a few minutes' walk. The hides are wooden tree-house structures perched on stilts overlooking grassy clearings or salt licks where animals come out under cover of darkness to replenish the minerals in their diet by licking the salt and minerals from the earth. These are safe and non-invasive methods of observing wildlife. Oblivious to being watched, the animals linger around the salt licks while you observe them. Animals like sambar deer, wild pigs, tapirs and occasionally, if you are very lucky, a *seladang*, herd of elephants and even a tiger might make an appearance.

Below: Wildlife observation from a jungle hide is a safe and great way of viewing animals, which are attracted to salt licks under cover of darkness.

Taman Negara National Park and Surrounds

Night Safari

Another intriguing way of watching wildlife is on a nocturnal jungle walk. There is something magical about walking in the darkness of the forest, guided only by the stars and serenaded by the night symphony of millions of cicadas and crickets, chirping in high crescendos competing with the croaks of frogs, then a shrill cry of some unknown creature in the dark. The jungle at night is noisy but the sound of nature is a balm to the soul. The jungle assumes a different persona as the coolness of night falls, the forest increasingly alive with myriad creatures prowling, foraging and hunting. The night walk is led by nature guides who are trained to detect even the slightest rustle in the jungle: the startled eyes of a sambar deer, or a slow loris perched high on a branch in the canopy. Bring a flashlight with you on the night walk.

The night safari in a 4-wheel-drive vehicle on oil palm plantation roads along the border of the forest is another excellent way to spot nocturnal creatures. Armed with a spotlight, the guide seeks out animals hunting. Wild boars, wild cats such as leopard and marble cats with beautiful marking, snakes curling on branches camouflaged among the leaves, a flying squirrel in flight, owls staring defiantly – these are all in a night's safari adventure.

Jungle Expeditions

Taman Negara's emerald forest is best explored on foot. Treks range from a short hike to arduous 9-day treks for die-hard jungle *wallahs*. Trekking trails are clearly marked and are safe and easy to follow if you keep to the marked trails. Do not wander off marked trails unless accompanied by guides. There are several trails, each has its own appeal and all are equally enchanting.

Canopy Walk

A visit to Taman Negara is not complete without a walk on this suspended walkway, 45m (148ft) above the forest floor. At 510m (558yd) long, it is the longest canopy walk in the world. It offers a spectacular view of the forest and a close-up view of the rich flora and fauna that flourish in the canopies of the giant rainforest trees. The suspension bridges and platforms were ecologically constructed by the Department of Wildlife and National Parks without nails, the trees protected with wooden frames fitted between the bark and the cables and ropes, thus avoiding any

Safety on a Canopy Walk

To ensure the safety of visitors while on the canopy walkway, the park authority has the following ten regulations:

1. Visitors are advised to be at least five metres away from each other while on the bridge (walkway).
2. Only four persons are allowed to be on each bridge at any one time.
3. Do not run on the bridge as this will cause it to sway.
4. Do not take any food and drinks onto the canopy walkway.
5. Do not stop for any undue length of time while on the canopy walkway.
6. Smoking is not permitted.
7. Do not carry sharp instruments, e.g. daggers or knives.
8. Do not vandalize or engrave on trees while on the platform.
9. Do not make noise.
10. You are requested to obey orders from the officer-in-charge.

There are altogether nine bridges and eight platforms along the 510m canopy walkway. Each bridge and platform bears descriptions of the trees and flora to observe.

Canopy Walk

Left: The Canopy Walkway at Taman Negara National Park is the longest in the world, offering visitors the thrilling experience of observing canopy birds and animals.

damage to the trees. Every measure is taken to protect the health of the trees and the visitors. The safety of visitors is of paramount importance and the walkways are inspected every morning before being opened to the public. The ropes have a minimum snapping strength of 5 tons and the steel cables more than 10 tons. Due to the height and rather wobbly nature of the aerial walkway, it is not recommended for those who fear heights. Opens Sat–Thu 11:00–15:00, Fri 09:00–12:00. Adults RM5 and children RM3.

The canopy walk can be combined with a trek to the Lubok Simpon trail, a picturesque spot for swimming, picnics and nature watching. The trail takes 4 hours, and Lubok Simpon is just 25 minutes from the park headquarters.

Bukit Teresek

Bukit Teresek lies 1.7km (1 mile) from the park headquarters. This popular trail starts with an easy flat terrain along the river embankment for 400m (437yd) then rises to a steep climb up to the Bukit Teresek ridge. There are two look-out points, one at each end of the ridge. The flat part of the trail passes through patches of tall forest, secondary forest, and scrub land, and is never far from the river. Birds indigenous to these habitats can

Taman Negara National Park and Surrounds

be found here, reputedly one of the best bird-watching areas in the park. The melodious song of the White-rumped Shama fills the air while the bubbling calls of Straw-headed Bulbuls echo along the river. The Greater Coucal's deep, mellow hoots can also be heard among the calls of the babblers, drongos, malkohas, hornbills and woodpeckers. As the paths increase in gradient through the tall forest, giant squirrels may be seen and occasionally white-handed gibbons. The first look-out point affords a panoramic view of the forested lowland and Sungai Tembeling, while the second look-out commands a wonderful vista of Sungai Tahan and the hills and mountains in the centre of the park. On a clear day, Gunung Tahan comes into view with its table-top profile. It is advisable to trek back to camp via the same route as the alternative route via Sungai Tahan is steep and can be treacherous when wet.

Lata Berkoh

A popular scenic spot worth visiting is the Lata Berkoh cataract on Sungai Tahan, 8.5km (5.3 miles) from Kuala Tahan. The river starts its source at Gunung Tahan and flows downstream in shallow water of less than 1m (3.3ft) deep forming a series of rapids and cascades over rocks and boulders. It is one of the most picturesque parts of Taman Negara, and the most popular for picnics and swimming. Water holes etched into the rocks by the force of water form natural Jacuzzis, ideal for cooling down in the jungle heat. The deep pools below the rapids look tempting for a swim but have very strong swirling currents and swimming is not advisable.

Below: Lata Berkoh's cataract of swirling pools and tumbling waters, ideal for water frolicks and picnicking.

For those who do not wish to do the 5-hour trek through the jungle to the cataract, a boat ride from Kuala Tahan along the navigable part of the river is a great opportunity to enjoy the beauty of the forest. The journey takes an hour depending on the level of the river; the boat travels

Gua Telinga

through enchanting riverine scenery along the narrow river with lovely close-up views of the riverine forest. The *neram* trees (*Dipterocarpus oblongifolius*), which grow in abundance on the river banks, form a natural archway over the river, creating a magical vista. The trunks and branches of the *neram* trees are clad with ferns and wild orchids. Birds along the river can include the handsome fish eagles, colourful kingfishers deftly diving for fish, vocal Straw-headed Bulbuls, and very occasionally the rare Masked Finfoot, much sought after by birders. There are very few water birds in the park. Mischievous macaques frolic in the trees while monitor lizards on the rocks bask in the sun. The boat stops 500m (547yd) below the cascade and a short trek along a path by the river takes you there. Boats can be booked through the Wildlife Department who control the boat hire at RM120 per boat for four people.

The Kelah Fish Sanctuary, the centre for research on sustainable conservation, is nearby. Game fishing at one time was one of the park's favourite activities and to prevent anglers from catching endangered species such as the kelah fish, licensed fishing is now confined to restricted areas in the national park. The large-scaled Kelah fish or Malaysian *mahseer*, a member of the carp family, can weigh up to 10kg (22lb). Visitors can feed the fish at the sanctuary, which has happily flourished after a decline from over-fishing.

Gua Telinga

There are several caves around the limestone hills of Taman Negara but the most popular is Ear Cave, or Gua Telinga in Malay. It is 2.6km (1.6 miles) from Kuala Tahan and takes about an hour and a half to walk to the cave, or a boat trip to the Gua jetty followed by a half-hour trek. Termite mounds can be seen along the way. A stream flows through several chambers of the cave with a rope to guide you on the 80m (87yd) route through the caves, following the stream. This cavernous and mysterious world takes about an hour to explore, at times crawling along narrow passages and negotiating areas knee-deep in slimy pungent guano. In some areas of the cave the passages are very narrow. The limestone cave supports a variety of wildlife such as roundleaf bats, dusky fruit bats, giant toads (some the size of a man's fist), black-striped frogs whose croaks can be heard echoing in the chambers, whip spiders, cave crickets, cockroaches, centipedes and racer snakes that feed on bats. The racer snake

Some Useful Malay Words

Perhilitan • Department of Wildlife and National Parks

Sungai/Sungei • River

Gunung • Mountain

Bukit • Hill

Lubuk • Natural pools found in rocks

Gua • Cave

Kuala • Coastal enclave

Taman Negara National Park and Surrounds

Shooting the Rapids

One of the highlights of visiting Taman Negara is shooting the rapids upstream from Kuala Tahan. The shallow waters of Sungai Tembeling flow through a gorge of sandstone rocks forming a series of seven whitewater rapids which can be negotiated under the guidance of skilful boatmen familiar with the churning waters. For the less daring there is the thrilling activity of rubber tubing, where you hurl your body onto a rubber tyre tube and float downstream through the rapids, defying the waters to do their worst. The rapids are not strong enough to cause danger and the bumpy ride through the fast-flowing water is an exhilarating experience. Life jackets will be supplied by the tour operators and must be worn at all times during the ride.

and the whip spider are not poisonous. Ancient drawings found on cave walls indicate early human settlement. Do not attempt to visit any caves alone and make sure you are equipped with a powerful torchlight or head lamp and, if possible, bring a spare one as well. The cave is pitch dark.

Gunung Tahan

The mighty Gunung Tahan lies 55km (34 miles) from the park headquarters in Kuala Tahan. To trek to the mountain takes 9 days and 8 nights, trekking over 27 hills to reach the summit at 2187m (7176ft). The journey takes you through wondrous forest with the vegetation and wildlife changing with the altitude. It is considered to be one of the toughest treks in Southeast Asia for mountain climbing, but many die-hard explorers have conquered the summit. Climbers should be physically and mentally equipped to handle this challenging expedition, not to mention the heat and humidity of a tropical forest. Experienced guides are essential for the journey.

Orang Asli Settlement

Orang Asli means 'Original People' in Malay and they are the aborigines of Malaysia. They are the oldest inhabitants of the Malay Peninsula. In Taman Negara, these forest people are known as the Negrito Batek. They lead a semi-nomadic lifestyle as hunter-gatherers, collecting fruits, wild yams and other jungle produce and hunting small mammals such as monkeys and squirrels with blow pipes. The Batek are a gentle race, short in stature, dark in appearance and with frizzy hair.They live in simple palm-thatched shelters, one for each family group, in a tight community. Their shelters can seen along some of the jungle trails. The men make a living as guides for Gunung Tahan expeditions in the park and their knowledge of the environment makes them excellent guides, sharing their intimate knowledge of the rainforest and their beliefs and customs that are central to their way of life. Their animistic world view encourages them to have a deep respect for nature.The Batek speak Malay as well as their own language. They welcome visitors to their settlement but respect for their privacy should be observed. Visitors should not just show up unannounced, and you should ask for permission before taking their pictures. Visits should be planned beforehand in consultation with the headman. The Batek are highly skilled in using the blow pipe and will sometimes demonstrate the art of using it to visitors and even invite them to try it out.

Getting There

There are four access points to Taman Negara: Kuala Tahan and Merapoh in Pahang, Kuala Koh in Kelantan and Tanjong Mentong in Terengganu. But the most convenient route for international visitors is from Kuala Lumpur. There are regular bus and taxi services from Pudu bus station in Kuala Lumpur to Jerantut, then another part taxi part bus ride to Kuala Tembeling jetty where the boats depart for Kuala Tahan.

The journey from Kuala Lumpur takes four hours to Jerantut and the boat ride is about three hours to Kuala Tahan. But as the journey is long and it can be complicated to co-ordinate the timing of public transport with the boat schedule, it would be advisable to book a package deal with experienced travel companies who could handle all the transfers, with a pick-up from your hotel all the way to your accommodation in Taman Negara, including meals, guides and excursions. Most travel companies operate tours to Taman Negara from Kuala Lumpur, including the following:

Asian Overland Services Tours and Travel,
Kuala Lumpur
tel: 603 4252 9100
e-mail: aos@asianoverland.com.my
website: www.asianoverland.com.my

Han Travel, Kuala Lumpur
tel: 603 2144 0899
e-mail: enquiry@taman-negara.com

Tahan Holidays, Kuala Lumpur
tel: 603 5636 0406
e-mail: info@tahan.com.my

Note: Taman Negara is a restricted conservation area and entry into the park requires an entry permit. All visitors should obtain their permits from the Department of Wildlife office at Kuala Tembeling jetty before

Below: Orang Asli of the Batek tribe, the jungle dwellers of the park, are skilled boatmen and their knowledge of the rivers and forests is unsurpassed.

Taman Negara National Park and Surrounds

Below: An A-frame chalet in the Taman Negara National Park. Much of the accommodation in the park consists of wooden buildings, in keeping with the natural environment.

embarking on the boat journey to Kuala Tahan. Passports (for foreign visitors) and two passport-sized photographs are required for the issuance of permits. A charge of RM5 is levied on each camera and/or piece of video equipment. The entrance fee to the park is RM1 per person.

Where To Stay

There are various grades of accommodation ranging from simple lodges and chalets to relatively luxurious hotels with all the mod-cons, all sympathetically constructed in wood in keeping with the environment of a national park. Budget hotels can be booked via travel companies who specialize in tours to Taman Negara and the more luxury grade hotels such as the Mutiara Taman Negara Resort and Rainforest Resort have their own sales office and tour packages including transfers from Kuala Lumpur.

Mutiara Taman Negara Resort

Built on 6ha (15 acres), Taman Negara Resort is an eco-tourism luxury resort with 108 rooms. It offers a variety of accommodation ranging from typical Malay timber chalets

Accommodation

(comprising Standard Chalets, Chalet Suites and Bungalows) to spacious motel-like guesthouses. Also available are dormitories, hostels and a 1ha (2.5-acre) camping ground.
tel: (609) 266 3500/2200
e-mail: fomtn@mutiarahotels.com
website: www.mutiarahotels.com

Rainforest Resort
The Rainforest Resort, located at Kuala Tahan village, offers medium range accommodation. All rooms are air-conditioned, with attached bathroom, hot shower, a private balcony, IDD telephone and a restaurant.
tel: (609) 266 7888/7241
e-mail: resvns@rainforest-tamannegara.com
website: www.rainforest-tamannegara.com

Woodland Resort
A short walk to the Park HQ, in Tahan Village. Accommodation in hotel-style block, wooden chalets and bungalows. All rooms have air conditioning and *en-suite* bathrooms.
tel: (609) 266 1111, e-mail: reservation@woodland.com.my
website: www.woodland.com.my

Teresek View
Teresek View is sited at Kuala Tahan village near the Taman Negara Park Headquarters within walking distance of the floating restaurant. It is another budget accommodation option offering simple but adequate amenities.
tel: (609) 266 9744
e-mail: infophg@yahoo.com
website: www.pahangtourism.com.my

Nusa Camp
Quaint guesthouse in Malay house style with air conditioning and *en-suite* bathroom.
tel: (609) 266 2369
e-mail: spkg@tm.net.my

Travellers' Home Taman Negara
This is budget accommodation, but it offers functional rooms with air conditioning.
tel: (609) 266 7766

Leeches

Leeches can be a problem on some jungle treks (about 50% of the time, especially after rain). They are not poisonous in themselves but their bites bleed and can become infected. The best way to deal with them is to flick them off clothing when first seen, to wear leech socks, or to touch them with a little dampened salt tied into the corner of a handkerchief. However, the odd leech may find its way on to your skin where it latches on and engorges itself with blood until satiated. It then releases itself and the small wound bleeds for a short time until the blood has clotted. Back at base the wound can be washed with antiseptic. Be careful not to scratch or the irritation may become annoying.

ENDAU ROMPIN NATIONAL PARK

Straddling the borders of the states of Johor and Pahang, Endau Rompin was the second national park to be established in Peninsular Malaysia after Taman Negara. The park takes its name from the watershed region of the Endau River in Johor and Rompin River in Pahang that flow through the park. The park is also served by two other rivers, Sungai Selai and Sungai Jasin.

Endau Rompin is one of the oldest primordial rainforests in the world. Steep cliffs, plateaus and deep gorges characterize the landscape, with rock formations dating back 250 million years. The undulating terrain of the region, its swampy enclaves and wooded valleys sweeping up to hilly ranges with elevations of over 900m (2953ft), supports a variety of forest types but primarily lowland and montane forest; it has one of the few remaining lowland forests in the country. Set against this background, Endau Rompin is an amazing adventure ground for nature-lovers and jungle-walkers to explore.

Top Ten

Giant Pitta
Grey-breasted Babbler
Kingfishers
Hornbills
Argus Pheasant
Tigers
Leopards
White-handed gibbons
Binturong
Tapirs

Opposite top: Sungai Endau, the lifeblood of the park, offers visitors riverine adventures.
Opposite centre: Among the amphibians found in Endau Rompin is the Spotted Litter Frog (Leptobrachium hendricksoni), which inhabits the leaf litter in primary forest.
Opposite bottom: Long boats transport visitors to the park, passing magnificent forest with views of birds and wildlife.

Endau Rompin National Park

History of Endau Rompin

Endau Rompin National Park

Location: 385km (239 miles) from Kuala Lumpur, about 5 hours.

Size: 900km² (347 sq miles).

Altitude: 900m (2953ft).

Of interest: Bird-watching, botany, nature study, rubber-tube rafting, jungle trekking, photography, river fording, night safari and a visit to an Orang Asli village.

The scientific study of the area was first conducted in 1892 by H W Lake, a miner and surveyor, accompanied by Lieutenant H J Kelsall. Their research led to the forested enclave of Endau Kluang being designated as a forest reserve in 1933, which later included the Lesong forest reserve in Pahang. It was discovered that the forest harbours the last few endangered Sumatran rhinoceros in the Malay Peninsula in addition to some very rare plants, but due to complications arising from federal and state legal rights in forest land, national park status could not be granted at the time. In the early 1980s when heavy logging in Johor threatened to ravage the forest, the Malaysian Nature Society launched the Scientific and Heritage Expedition to save the forest and mobilized the public to set up funds for their scientific expedition. Individuals, local companies and organizations provided sponsorship for this huge undertaking. More than seventy Malaysian scientists as well as nearly one thousand students and volunteers enrolled to be part of the campaign. During their exploration from 1984 to 1989, they discovered 25 new species of plants of which half are endemic. They also discovered that the biodiversity and species of the forest were more than originally anticipated. In the same year, the government of Johor finally allowed 251.95km² (97 sq miles) of the area to be gazetted as a national park. The national park was further enlarged after Pahang and Johor came to an agreement. The Endau Rompin National Park was officially gazetted in 1993 with a total area of approximately 900km² (347 sq miles) of forest land of which 489km² (189 sq miles) is in Johor and the rest in Pahang.

Flora and Fauna

The park is home to some of the most endangered animals in Malaysia and several endemic plants. Pitcher plants (*Nepenthes*), some borne of aerial stems, grow in the montane forest, as do a variety of orchids, herbs of the African violet family and medicinal plants used by the Orang Asli forest people. The largest and most spectacular plant is the *Livistona endauensis*, the elegant fan-palm, believed to be endemic to this park. It grows in abundance on the Gunung Janing Barat plateau. Others include climbing bamboo (*Rhopa coblaste*) and walking stick palm (*Phychorapis singaporensis*) – a slender stem palm with feather-like fronds.

Jungle Adventures

Fauna includes the endangered Sumatran rhinoceros, tigers, elephants and leopards which are rarely seen. Other animals found here are tapirs, leaf monkeys, long-tail macaques, white-handed gibbons, lesser mousedeer, binturong and sambar deer. White-handed gibbons are the only type of ape found in this park. The binturong belongs to the civet family and is also known as the bearcat due to its bear-like appearance. It has dark, coarse fur and a long, bushy prehensile tail that helps it to manoeuvre in the treetops. The lesser mousedeer is tiny, barely 30cm (12in) tall, and is known as *sang kancil* (a mythical mousedeer in popular Malay folklore) for its guile and craftiness. It is commonly spotted in lowland forest, especially on night safaris. Over 250 species of birds are found here, including *Picumnus innominatus* (the Speckled Piculet, one of the smallest woodpeckers in the world – the size of a human thumb), the rare Giant Pitta, Grey-breasted Babbler, eagles, kingfishers, hornbills and a variety of species indigenous to the lowland and montane forests.

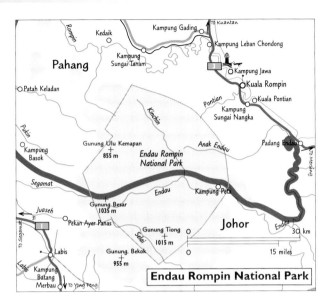

Jungle Adventures

Endau Rompin, with its limited infrastructure, is not suitable for luxury-seeking visitors but is rewarding for nature-lovers who are prepared to sacrifice creature comfort to have the privilege of immersing themselves in riverine adventures and jungle exploits. Popular activities include camping, swimming, bird-watching, botany, fishing, photography, jungle trekking and river fording.

Jungle Trekking

The park has 26km (16 miles) of jungle trails. Four camp sites cater for 250 to 300 visitors, located at Kuala Jasin, Batu Hampar, Upeh Guling and Kuala Marong along with a variety of treks.

Endau Rompin National Park

Opposite: A scenic waterfall on the Jasin River in the park; the cool, clear water is perfect for cooling down and swimming amid the sounds and sights of nature.

Buaya Sangkut, The Trapped Crocodile

The Orang Asli have many legends relating to the various spots in the forest. The most popular one is the waterfall at Buaya Sangkut, which means 'Trapped Crocodile' in Malay. Legend has it that once upon a time, the River Jasin and River Endau were infested with crocodiles, endangering the lives of the people in the area who lived in fear of the ferocious reptiles. The Orang Asli believed that the only way to allay their fear was to kill the King Crocodile. One day they caught the crocodile and hurled it down the waterfall and it became trapped under the rocks and drowned. Since then the waterfall has been referred to as 'Buaya Sangkut.' It is believed that when the water level at the waterfall is low during the dry season, a crocodile-shaped rock can be seen in the swirls of the water.

Buaya Sangkut Camp Site (advanced trek)

The most famous trail is the challenging 16km (10-mile) Kuala Jasin to Batu Hampar and Buaya Sangkut trail involving numerous fordings over fast flowing rivers. The total trekking time is about 6–10 hours. The 2.2km (1.4-mile) trek to Buaya Sangkut is a gruelling 2½ hours' trek from Batu Hampar. The journey begins with a half-hour meander through gentle grounds with large umbrella palms (*Johannesteysmannia altifrons*) shading the way. The first stop is at the base of Bukit Segongong, at 765m (2510ft). The climb rises at a 60° incline almost all the way. It can get slippery when the ground is wet but there are rattan ropes for support. Bring plenty of drinking water and some light energy-boosting snacks. All the hard trekking is made worthwhile upon reaching Buaya Sangkut. The waterfall is 300m (984ft) above sea level on Sungai Jasin and is 40m (131ft) high and 30m (98ft) wide, with about 80m³ (about 17,000 gallons) of water hurtling down every second over a drop of 120m (394ft). Along the river's edge in calm water, prawns can be seen darting from under pebbles in search of food. Buaya Sangkut is a stunning spot to admire nature while at the same time being refreshed by its cool waters.

Batu Hampar Campsite (intermediate trek)

About 4 hours of moderate walking from Kuala Jasin through fairly flat terrain, Batu Hampar is the pit stop before making the ascent to the Buaya Sangkut waterfall. Not far from Batu Hampar is another waterfall, the Upeh Guling. Here, roaring cascades spurt and surge downwards, tumbling into the waterfall. Several natural 'Jacuzzis' are found in this area, believed to have been formed by tiny pebbles lodged in crevices that whirled round and round by the force of water, boring holes into the rocks over millions of years. These natural swirl holes are nicknamed 'guling-guling' or 'rolling round and round' in Malay. Upeh Guling Falls, which derived its name from this Orang Asli legend, is the best place to go for a swim.

Kuala Marong Camp Site (beginners' trek)

This is a leisurely 2-hour trek from Kuala Jasin Base Camp. Kuala Marong is the perfect camp site for trekkers who do not mind roughing it and can endure the back-to-nature basic facilities. There are freshwater fish nurseries in the nearby tranquil pools,

Jungle Adventures

with various species including the
protected Kelah (Malaysian mahseer
carp) and patin cat fish. Upriver, about
50m (55yd) away at the turn of the
river, a crystal clear pool called 'Tasik
Air Biru', or blue lagoon, is a great
place for swimming.

Orang Asli Village

Endau Rompin is home to the Orang
Asli of the Jakun tribe. Traditionally
they live a nomadic life living off the
land and, like all the Orang Asli
people, they are hunter-gatherers.
Their unsurpassed knowledge of the
forest and its flora and fauna makes
them excellent guides around the
parks. Jungle produce (like fruits, yams
and tapioca) and small animals provide
their staple diet, while the abundant
supply of fish in the Endau River supplements their food larder.
They are skilled at identifying medicinal plants and herbs for
curing illness and the community has their own shaman to look
after their health. A walk through the park with a Jakun guide will
open up a whole new world of forest secrets and even magic as
he regales visitors with the tribe's myths and legends. For the past
17 years, the Jakuns in Endau Rompin have been re-settled by the
government at Kampung Peta, a village near the park entry point.
They are engaged in agricultural activities such as growing rubber
and fruit trees like rambutans and durians, two favourite local
fruits. Visitors are welcome in their village to observe their
lifestyle and learn of their mythological tales, but it is important to
respect their privacy and, unless invited, it is not polite to enter
their homes or take their pictures without permission.

Nature Walk

Endau Rompin is endowed with stunning natural vistas of soaring
hills and cliffs punctuated by rivers, tumbling cascades and
waterfalls. While it is not easy to spot animals in the dense
vegetation of the forest, the sheer sweep of beauty filled with

Upeh Guling Falls Legend

This beauty spot is named after a
rather bizarre Orang Asli legend. It
was said that a young Orang Asli
was on his way to a cockfight when
he was startled to see his lovely lady
by the water edge. When he spun
round to greet her, he slipped and
fell, rolling round and round against
the rocks into the waterfall, and
died. Hence the waterfall is named
after the tragic accident of this
young man.

Endau Rompin National Park

Right: Mussaenda mutabilis —
the star-shaped orange flower
adds a touch of colour to the
forest, filling the air with its
intoxicating fragrance.

melodious birdsong is a reminder that national parks like these should be protected in perpetuity for future generations. Given the diverse variety of plant and animal species and habitats in the area, nature walking is particularly fulfilling here. Inhale the intoxicating fragrance of the *Mussaenda mutabilis*, a woody climbing plant of the *Rubiaceae* family with orange, star-shaped, fragrant flowers, used in olden days for scenting hair and clothes. Watch out for colourful butterflies perched on the *Melostoma* plant with its purple blooms and sweet buds, often used in traditional medicine. In the montane habitat, observe a pitcher plant in action trapping unwary insects in its water-filled cups, or be fascinated by a colony of ants emerging in a regimental line from the 'ant plant' (*Hydnophytum formicarium*) which provides internal chambers for the ants' nest in return for their protection of the host plant from attack by plant-eating insects.

Fishing

Some of the best fishing spots in Malaysia can be found in Endau Rompin National Park. The most popular sites are along the lower reaches of Sungai Kinchin and Sungai Kemapan. The best times for fishing are February to April and June to August. Fishing is prohibited from September to October during the spawning season to allow the fish population to regenerate.

Park Regulations

Park Regulations

1. All visitors are required to report to the officer on duty at the Registration Centre in Kampung Peta.

2. There will be a short briefing at the Registration Centre. Entrance and other prescribed fees will be collected. All items and belongings are inspected by the officer on duty.

3. Visitors are not allowed to stay in the park beyond the specified period.

4. All visitors are required to engage the registered guides of the National Parks Corporation.

5. Visitors who wish to hire boat services can inquire from the officer on duty.

6. Visitors are prohibited from making unnecessary noise while in the park to avoid disturbance to wildlife.

7. All empty cans, surplus food and rubbish have to be taken out of the park, and disposed of at designated disposal areas.

8. Entry into the park is only allowed through the specified entrances as determined by the National Park.

9. No fishing or angling is allowed in the park except at specified areas and times.

10. Bathing and swimming are only allowed at specified areas – swimmers must be in decent swimming attire.

11. The National Parks Corporation disclaims responsibility for any mishap, accident or loss of belongings of any visitor while in the park.

12. Visitors are strictly forbidden from :

• Bringing into the park any machinery, weapon, explosive, trap, poison or dangerous item.

• Hunting, killing, hurting, trapping, or disturbing any flora/fauna, habitat or destroying birds' nests and eggs.

• Chopping, hurting, destroying or burning any plants and other objects that have geological, archaeological, historical or scientific importance.

• Carrying into or purposely allowing reared domestic animals to enter the park.

• Displacing or moving any animals or plants, dead or alive, out of the park.

• Displacing or moving out of the park any minerals or objects of geological, archaeological, historical or scientific importance.

• Erecting any building in the park.

Fees at the Park

Guide: RM 50.00 per day (one guide per 10 visitors) Compulsory for all visitors.

Entry permit for Zone A (can be paid at the park): RM20.00

Entry permit for Zone B: (can be paid at the park) RM20.00

Tent and camp: RM12.50 per person per day

Insurance: RM1.50 per person per day

Camera: RM10.00

Video camera: RM 50.00 per unit

Filming: RM1000.00 per day

Fishing permit: RM20.00 per fishing rod. Fishing is allowed at the designated area only.

Endau Rompin National Park

For information on the Park and permits, please enquire with:

Johor National Park Corporation (PTNJ), JKR 475, Bukit Timbalan, 80000 Johor Baharu, Johor Darul Takzim;

tel: 607 223 7471 or 224 2525

fax: 607 223 7472

e-mail: ptnj@po.jaring.my

website: www.johorparks.com

Visitors to the park are warned that they are liable to be prosecuted in the event they are found to have contravened any of the park regulations.

Getting there

From Kuala Lumpur or Johor Bahru, travel by the North-South Highway. On reaching Kluang, detour to Kahang town. There, a four-wheel-drive vehicle will take you on a 56km (35-mile) jungle track to Kampung Peta, the Visitors' Centre and the point of entry to the National Park. Alternatively it is a 3-hour journey by boat from Felda Nitar II.

There are three entry points to the park: Kampung Peta, Nitar and West entry. The former is located 56km (35 miles) from Pahang. Visitors have to travel through rubber and oil palm plantations as well as dense jungle along dirt tracks to the base camp. From Nitar, a Felda Plantation agriculture scheme, the park can be reached after an 8-hour boat ride along the Endau River. Kampung Peta is also the most remote Orang Asli (aboriginal) settlement in Johor.

Entry permits are required for those wishing to visit the park, and additional charges are levied for entry into specific zones within the park. There are also charges for filming and fishing equipment. Travelling independently can be quite complicated due to the limited infrastructure of Endau Rompin. It is advisable to book a tour package from tour companies who will arrange everything from permit to transport, accommodation, guide and excursions. Note that the park is closed during the rainy season from November to March.

The following travel companies operate tours to the park:

Journey Malaysia, Kuala Lumpur
tel: 603 2692 8049
e-mail: pappy@journeymalaysia.com
website: www.journeymalaysia.com

Capslock Travel Management, Kuala Lumpur
tel: 603 9171 7852

Accommodation

e-mail: infocentre@abcmalaysia.com
website: www.abcmalaysia.com

Pure Value Travel and Tours, Mersing, Johor
tel: 607 799 6811
website: www.purevalue.com.my

Where to Stay

Endau Rompin is fairly underdeveloped with limited infrastructure and the limited accommodations are very basic. It is only recommended for those who are prepared to rough it.

Kampung Peta

The park is at its early stages of building facilities for visitors. However, there are basic A-frame huts available at Kampung Peta's staging point. Running water and flushing toilets are available at the Park Headquarters and a provision shop is opened during the day, which sells packets of noodles and snacks.

Kuala Jasin

Basic A-frame huts and camp site available, toilet and piped water.

Kuala Marong

Basic thatched hut available, and camp site.

For enquiries on these accommodations and also transportation,
tel: 607 223 7471 or
607 224 2525,
fax: 607 223 7472,
e-mail: jnpc@johorpark.com
website: www.johorparks.com
or else you can make your booking through a travel company.

Below: The macho rhinoceros beetle is just one of the many weird and wonderful insects found in the forest.

ROYAL BELUM STATE PARK AND TEMENGOR FOREST RESERVE

The Royal Belum State Park is the latest addition to Malaysia's cache of wild assets. Its ecological treasure trove remained undiscovered for many years when the area was classified as high security risk zone during the communist insurgency. Today, with its pristine virgin forest teeming with wildlife, rare plants and a vast picturesque lake, it is the perfect setting for jungle sojourns. The open waters are excellent for fishing, canoeing and lake safaris to observe wildlife and birds along the lake, while the lush forest and scenic spots are ideal for photography, camping, jungle trekking and bird-watching. All ten species of Malaysian hornbills are found here, and highly endangered mammal species such as the clouded leopard and Malayan tiger have been recorded in the park though they are rarely spotted. It is poised to become Malaysia's latest retreat for nature-lovers.

Top Ten

Plain Pouched Hornbill
Wreathed Hornbill
Bushy-crested Hornbill
Kingfishers
Trogons
Asian elephants
Seladang
Malayan tiger
Sun bear
Clouded leopard

Opposite top: Calotes emma, *an agamid lizard, is one of many reptiles found in Belum.*
Opposite centre: A tranquil *scene – Temengor Lake surrounded by lush forest and mountain ranges.*
Opposite bottom: A road sign *warning motorists of elephants crossing the highway.*

Royal Belum State Park & Temengor Forest Reserve

Royal Belum State Park and Temengor Forest Reserve

The Belum and Temengor forest was given the royal warrant by the Sultan of Perak, Sultan Azlan Shah, when he declared it the 'Royal Belum Park' in July 2003, but it was not given the protected status of a state park. The riches of the forest would have been threatened if not for the unrelenting campaign by NGOs such as WWF Malaysia and the Malaysian Nature Society (MNS) who were pivotal in lobbying for the area to be protected. The MNS conducted two main expeditions in the area, one in 1993 and one in 1998, in their 'Belum-Temengor Forest Complex Conservation Initiative' campaign. Their study found that this nature treasure house supports a rich biodiversity of flora and fauna and further destruction of its natural resources could lead to the loss of 'future opportunities these forests possess in biotechnology, pharmacology and nature tourism'.

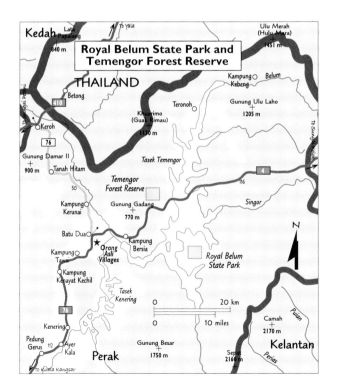

It was a victory for MNS, who successfully persuaded the Perak state government to designate Belum as a forest reserve, and on 3 May 2007, it was officially gazetted as Royal Belum State Park. The park is managed by Perak State Parks Corporation. An area of 117,500ha (290,343 acres) was conserved and proclaimed as a no-logging zone, representing a quarter of the total area of 280,000ha (691,880 acres) that MNS had originally campaigned for. However, the Temengor Forest Reserve remains unprotected and logging still continues, although the Perak state government has declared that logging in the area will cease by 2008.

Nature's Treasure House of the North

Nature's Treasure House of the North

Belum forest is the northernmost frontier of Perak, abutting the border with Thailand and spanning a vast area of 2000km² (772 sq miles), of which 117,500ha (290,343 acres) of pristine tropical rainforest are designated as a state park. The forest is dominated by the huge man-made Temengor Lake and Hydro Electric Dam, fed by many waterways, as well as meadow land and some abandoned agricultural plots. The rocky, undulating landscape straddling the Titiwangsa Main Range midway between the west and east coasts gives rise to luxuriant forests, which include lowland dipterocarp, hill dipterocarp and lower montane types. The Royal Belum State Park is part of the larger Belum-Temengor forest complex, one of the largest tracts of forest in Peninsular Malaysia. It is in fact the green lungs of northern Malaysia and a focal survival point for the wildlife and people of the forest. Its unspoiled primary forest is of great biological significance and supports a vast ecosystem of flora and fauna, of which 100 mammals have been recorded. There are many rare and endangered species such as the seladang, Asian elephant and Malayan tiger. The area is also home to the endangered Sumatran rhinoceros, one of very few left in Peninsular Malaysia. WWF Malaysia is working on the Honda Rhino Project to study and conserve the species in Belum. Other species found here are sun bear; serow; rare felines such as wild fishing cats who fish with their paws by the stream, the illusive clouded leopards, black panthers and various species of wild cats; numerous snake species and other reptiles; flying foxes, bats, otters, porcupines, pangolins and many other creatures of the rainforest. Belum has 200 species of butterflies, 274 bird species and thousands of insects and invertebrates. The forest teems with life, something you will realize when you stop, on a trek, to savour the sound, sight and smell of the forest. The cacophony of chirping insects and the chorus of birdsong fill the air, while the shrieks of primates can be heard among the trees.

Belum-Temengor forest complex is the only forest in Malaysia which is home to all 10 species of Malaysian hornbills, namely the Wrinkled Hornbill, White-crowned Hornbill, Wreathed Hornbill, Plain-pouched Hornbill, Helmeted Hornbill, Great Hornbill, Rhinoceros Hornbill, Bushy-crested Hornbill, Oriental Pied

Royal Belum State Park and Temengor Forest Reserve

Location: 300km (190 miles) from Kuala Lumpur.
Size: 117,500ha (290,343 acres).
Of interest: Angling, canoeing, a visit to an Orang Asli settlement, nature watching and jungle trekking.

Royal Belum State Park & Temengor Forest Reserve

Hornbill and Black Hornbill. Large flocks of endangered Plain-pouched Hornbills and Wreathed Hornbills are often seen gathering around fruit trees or roosting in raucous groups, normally between the months of July and November. A record number of over 2000 Plain-pouched Hornbills have been recorded by MNS in one evening, an occurrence never before seen in other parks in Malaysia. Hornbills are reputedly the barometer of the health of a forest and this phenomenon is an indication that the Belum-Temengor forest complex is in great shape and should be conserved in its entirety rather than in fragmented enclaves.

Large mammals are seldom encountered on jungle trekking and they tend to retreat deep into the forest. Evidence of the presence of elephants, seladang, wild boars, tigers, tapir and deer is often found at salt licks scattered round the forest, but the animals are seldom seen. Overnight stays at simple observation huts at salt licks can be arranged through the resorts and local tour companies to see animals at night. On rare occasions, the Orang Asli people living in the area have spotted tigers in the wild. The shy animals have not been a threat to humans as their territories to date have not been threatened. Tigers are highly territorial animals and it is imperative that the natural habitat of this dwindling species is protected.

There are over 3000 species of plant in the forest including many medicinal plants and herbs, commonly used by the Orang Asli to make into lotions and potions to cure sickness, for health nutrients and even as aphrodisiacs. The forest is the world's natural medicine cabinet. Studies are continuously being undertaken by scientists to research deeper into the healing properties of these medicinal plants.

The forest is particularly rich in fruit trees such as rambutans, mangoes, jackfruits, wild lemons and figs. The fruits are favourites with birds, long-tailed and pig-tailed macaques, gibbons and squirrels. Wild boars, porcupines and other ground animals feed on fallen fruits shaken from the trees by the monkeys, and even insects feed on them. Fruit trees in fact support a whole array of wildlife.

People of the Forest

The forest hardwoods, such as meranti, cengal, keruing and the merbau species, have become increasingly rare due to logging. Exotic plant species like wild ginger, orchids, ferns, bamboo and tongkat ali, a plant that purportedly possesses aphrodisiac value, grow in profusion in the dense humid jungle. Four species of rafflesia are found here, including *Rafflesia azlanii*, named after Sultan Azlan of Perak.

Above: In 2004 the Malayan tiger was recognized as a new subspecies and given the name Panthera tigris jacksoni. It is estimated that fewer than 500 now exist in the wild.

People Of The Forest

There are 18 indigenous tribes or Orang Asli in Peninsular Malaysia, two of whom live in the Belum-Temengor forest reserve. There are estimated to be about 5600 Orang Asli living in the area. These are the Jahai, a sub-ethnic group of the Negritos, and the Temiar, a main tribe of the Senoi group. The Jahai people have a Negroid appearance with dark skin and Afro

Royal Belum State Park & Temengor Forest Reserve

hair. The men are stockily built and are skilled hunters and gatherers. The Temiar tend to be gentle and shy and live as a close community, sharing what they have equally among themselves. Most Temiar have been converted to Islam but some have retained their belief in animism, the worship of spirits in nature. They live spiritual and mystical lives and believe that dreams augur their souls' journey in this world through their spirit guides. These two tribes were once semi-nomadic forest-dwellers but are now housed in government-built villages around Temengor Lake, which was flooded to construct the Hydro Electric Dam in 1975.

When the dam was built, the whole valley was flooded, creating 18,000ha (44,478 acres) of lake measuring 80km (50 miles) long, 5km (3 miles) wide and 124m (407ft) in its deepest part. The Orang Asli villages of Kampong Temengor along with their ancestral burial grounds were submerged. Four hundred villagers were relocated to government-built settlements by the lake. The flood created 80 small islands out of the 80 hills that were part of the landscape of the valley. The water teems with fish, particularly around the tributaries – a source of food for the residents and angling for tourists. Small communities of Orang Asli have resisted living in modern houses and choose to live in traditional thatched dwellings on some of the islands and at the edge of the forest, eking a living from tourism, as guides and jungle scouts, as well as selling fruits and handicrafts. They mainly live off the land, however, using their unsurpassed knowledge of the forest and their survival skills in the wild.

Below: Porcupines are regularly seen at night in Malaysian forests and are the fourth largest rodents in the world. Their bodies are clad in long quills which they use as body armour to protect themselves against predators.

Places of Interest and Activities

Tourism in the Belum-Temengor park is in its infancy and infrastructure is still fairly underdeveloped, with simple but comfortable accommodation and camping facilities. But it is this unspoilt aspect that makes the park special and perfect for hardcore nature lovers who come to experience the magic of the forest. Activities include fishing, canoeing, bird-watching and boat trips round the lake to visit the islands. Banding Island, in the middle of the lake, has a resthouse (the Banding Island Resort, see below) and a petrol station. There are indoor and outdoor activities on the island, including fishing, bird-watching, jungle trekking and boating. Banding Island is also the venue of the annual Banding Fishing Contest.

Pulau (Island) Bubung, Pulau Chiong, Pulau Tekam and Pulau Tujuh are some of the many islands in Lake Temengor that are inhabited by the Jahai and Temiar indigenous people. They welcome visitors to their settlements and are happy to talk about their lifestyle, beliefs and legends, and will also demonstrate their blow pipe technique and rattan handicraft-making. It is important to respect their privacy and customs and, if possible, to make prior arrangements.

The waters around the islands are great locations for freshwater fishing, one of the main activities in this park. There are various trails to explore in the jungle, but for security reasons, all trekkers must be accompanied by guides who will register your names at Kampong Chiong before setting off. There are tranquil lagoons and cascading waterfalls in which to swim during the treks and many new and wonderful creatures to behold. The magic of Belum unfolds the moment you step into its domain.

Getting There and Accommodation

Royal Belum State Park is located in northern Perak. The nearest towns are Grik in Perak and Jeli in Kelantan in the north. Traversing the scenic East-West Highway, the journey from Kuala Lumpur to Belum takes about six hours. It is advisable to book your trip to the area through tour operators as they will arrange all transfers, accommodation and permits for the park. Banding Island Resort has 28 air-conditioned rooms with en-suite bathrooms, a restaurant and function rooms that can accommodate 10 to 150 people.

Contact: Journey Malaysia, Kuala Lumpur, tel: 603 2692 8049, e-mail: pappy@journeymalaysia.com
Website: www.journeymalaysia.com

Malayan Tiger (*Panthera tigris jacksoni*)

The tiger is the largest of the world's four big cats, the other three being the lion, leopard and jaguar. Native to mainland Southeast Asia, the tiger is at the top of the food chain in the jungle. It is highly endangered due to its perceived value in Chinese traditional medicine, and tigers in the wild continue to be poached. Most of the world's tigers now live in captivity in zoos, tiger sanctuaries or in private collections. The tiger is a solitary animal and highly defensive of its territory. It prefers to live in dense forest, as in the case of the Malayan tiger. The male tiger is much larger than the female and has a wider home range. Tigers hunt by stalking and pouncing on their prey, breaking their necks and puncturing their windpipes. Their orange and black stripes are unique to each animal, much as fingerprints are to humans. The Malayan tiger was only recognized as a subspecies in its own right in 2004 and it has now been renamed *Panthera tigris jacksoni*. A recent count reveals that there are only 400–500 tigers in the wild in Malaysia. It is the national emblem of Malaysia – the coat of arms bears two tigers holding up a shield topped by a crescent moon and star – and it symbolizes bravery and strength.

BAKO, KUBAH & GUNUNG GADING NATIONAL PARKS

With its rich natural heritage, Sarawak has gazetted several prime virgin forests as national parks and forest reserves, boasting eighteen national parks, four wildlife sanctuaries and five nature reserves, a total area of 512,387.47ha (1,266,109 acres), making it one of the most extensive protected area networks in Malaysia.

Sarawak sits on the northwest coast of Borneo occupying 12,444km² (4803 sq miles) of land area with 800km (500 miles) of coastline, its southernmost tip just one degree north of the equator. It is the largest state in Malaysia, making up over a third of the country's landmass, but home to only a tenth of the nation's population of 24.8 million. Its proximity to the equator gives it rainfall throughout the year with relatively heavier rainfall from September to March.

Top Ten

Sea Eagles
Hornbills
Velvet-fronted Nuthatch
Racket-tailed Drongo
Sunbirds
Otters
Long-tailed macaques
Bornean bearded pigs
Proboscis monkeys
Flying lemur

Opposite, top to bottom:
The famous sea stack, the icon of Bako National Park; the mudskipper, a fish that can breathe on land, is often seen loitering on the muddy banks of the mangrove thickets at Bako National Park; monitor lizards are commonly spotted basking in the sun on rocks along the coastline of the park.

Bako, Kubah and Gunung Gading National Parks

Sarawak

Dolphins

There are nine species of dolphins along the coastal waters of Sarawak and they are under the Totally Protected Animals Act. The inshore species are Irrawaddy Dolphins, Finless Porpoise and Indo-Pacific Humpbacked Dolphin. The offshore or marine dolphins are Bottlenose Dolphin, Pantropical Spotted Dolphin, Risso's Dolphin, Fraser's Dolphin or Sarawak Dolphin, Common Dolphin and Killer Whale. In Kuching, these mammals can be spotted along the Salak River, Santubong estuary and at the Bako-Buntal Bay. Irrawaddy Dolphins are the most commonly found dolphins in the bay and best time to see them is between May and October.

Sarawak has a rich heritage of natural and biological diversity to rival any of the world's nature reserves, making it a premier area for endemic flora and fauna. It is estimated that Sarawak has more than 8000 species of flowering plants; 2000 species of vertebrates; 10,000 species of invertebrates; 757 species of ferns; and 4500 species of fungi in the forests.

The fauna can be broken down to 185 species of mammals, 560 species of birds, 166 species of snakes, 104 of lizards and 113 of amphibians. A large proportion of Sarawak's animals are unique to Borneo and do not occur in mainland Southeast Asia. These include approximately 19% of the mammals, 6% of the birds, 20% of the snakes and 32% of the lizards, all largely found in 'Totally Protected Areas'. The vascular flora of Sarawak comprises more than 8000 species. Over 2000 tree species have been enumerated whereas orchid types number more than 1000 species. Ferns account for 757 species and palms make up another 260 species.

Bako National Park

Bako National Park is Sarawak's most popular coastal national park, covering an area of 2727ha (6738 acres) of nature reserve, that in its diversity represents a microcosm of Sarawak's vegetation. Gazetted as a protected area on 1 May 1957 when Sarawak was still a colony of the British Empire, it is the oldest national park in the state. Its location at the rocky headland of the Muara Tebas Peninsula gives Bako National Park a unique coastline of sandstone cliffs, sandy beaches and mangrove swamps. Its hilly interior and varied topography accommodate all the forest types in the state. The park is 30km (19 miles) from Kuching, the capital city of Sarawak, and getting there entails a 45-minute drive from the city followed by a 30-minute boat ride from Kampung Bako, the village from which the park got its name.

The introduction to the park's vegetation begins with a boat ride that will take you through the mouth of the Bako River, with its banks lined by nipah palms and mangrove trees. As the boat approaches the park, you can see the sandstone cliffs rising from the sandy beaches and the mangrove and nipah give way to beach vegetation and mixed dipterocarp forest stretching inland from

Bako National Park

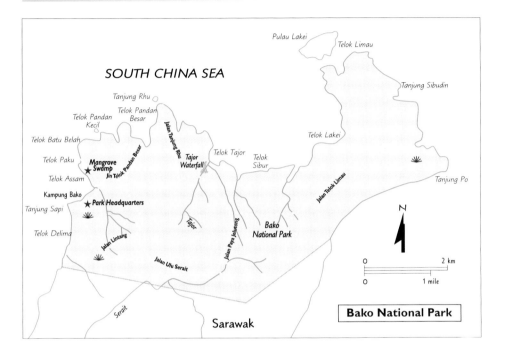

SOUTH CHINA SEA

Pulau Lakei
Telok Limau
Tanjung Sibudin
Tanjung Rhu
Telok Pandan
Besar
Telok Pandan
Kecil
Telok Batu Belah
Telok Lakei
Telok Paku
Mangrove
Swamp
Telok Tajor
Tajor
Waterfall
Telok
Sibur
Jin Telok
Telok Assam
Tanjung Po
Kampung Bako
Park Headquarters
Tanjung Sapi
Telok Delima
Bako
National Park
Jalan Lintang
Jalan Ulu Serait
Serait
Sarawak

N

0 ——— 2 km
0 ——— 1 mile

Bako National Park

the top of low cliffs. Landing at Telok Assam (Assam Bay) near the Park Headquarters after a short ride in the open sea, you disembark at a jetty in the middle of a mangrove swamp forest.

Your adventure in observing nature begins the very moment you land at the park. One of the first creatures you will encounter are the mudskippers, slimy fish with bulging eyes at the top of their heads. They can breathe out of water as they loiter on the mudflats or skip away from the boat.

At the muddy banks of the small river that runs through the park into the bay among the protruding roots of the mangrove trees are numerous small crabs scavenging for food. The most colourful are the male fiddler crabs with their blue and orange oversized pincers, which although looking like formidable weapons are in fact used primarily to attract female crabs. On the swampy banks, monitor lizards, which can grow up to 2m (6.6ft) long, can often be spotted basking in the sun. Troupes of long-tailed macaques

**Bako
National Park**

Location: 30km (19 miles) from Kuching. Flight from Kuala Lumpur to Kuching is 1 hour 45 minutes.
Size: 2727ha (6738 acres).
Of interest: Bird-watching, trekking, night safari, photography, beachcombing and nature watch.

Bako, Kubah and Gunung Gading National Parks

often romp among the mangroves, occasionally venturing down to the mudflats to catch a crab or pick up shellfish. Kingfishers perched on branches scan the water below, ready to swoop down on any unwary fish.

Bako is the best place to observe animals in the wild. After many years of protection from hunting, the animals here, although still shy, are less wary of human presence, some so familiar with visitors that they venture very close to the lodges, cafeteria and the Park Headquarters. In fact, you have to keep a lookout for the pestiferous long-tailed macaques, which are apt to steal anything you leave unattended, while the Bornean bearded wild pigs can get uncomfortably close as they look for food leftovers near lodges or the canteen. The pigs are so named because of the prominent bristles on either side of their snout. They are the biggest animals in the park. The gentle silvered leaf monkeys are also usually found among the trees near both the canteen and park offices, while monitor lizards amble nonchalantly close only to dart away at any sudden movement.

Below: The Malayan flying lemur (Cynocepahlus variegatus), a species of the Colugo family, is often seen gliding from tree to tree at Bako National Park.

There are two species of otter in the park: the oriental small-clawed otter and the hairy-nosed otter. They can be seen swimming in streams or scurrying across the mudflats looking for fish and crustaceans. Besides the monitor lizards, other lizards commonly found in the park are the skink or sun lizard, usually found sunning itself on rocks, and the green crested lizard perched on the branches of the trees. A flying lizard will occasionally launch itself gliding from tree to tree. The best times to observe animals are early morning and towards evening as the animals are most active during these times.

For ardent bird-watchers, Bako is an excellent spot; 150 species of birds have been recorded here. You can see quite a few of them near the rest houses and around the park offices, and one of the best spots to watch birds is at Telok Assam, the landing point at the jetty. However, you will have to hit the trails to appreciate the variety of species in the park. One rare animal species to look out for is the proboscis monkey, which is found only in Borneo. You can see them at Telok Assam especially towards the late afternoon although you might have to take one of the trails to catch a better glimpse of them, usually high in the trees feeding on leaves.

While there is plenty of life in the daytime, the cacophony of insects shrills, hooting of owls, croaking of tree frogs and calls of nocturnal animals heralds another busy time in the forest as nocturnal animals come out to forage for food when darkness descends. These include the flying lemur, mousedeer, tarsier, slow loris, pangolin, civets and bats. You might catch a glimpse of some them scurrying on the forest floor on a night walk near the park office. If you shine a torch up into the trees you are likely to catch the reflection of some animal's eyes among the branches; these are usually the slow loris, tarsier or the civet, which are more comfortable in the foliage than on the ground. There is also a wide variety of snakes, most of them non-venomous. The snakes commonly seen at the park are the grass green whip snake and the paradise tree snake. The Wagler's pit viper is the only snake classified as poisonous.

A walk along the beach and the edge of the mangrove swamp is also an enriching experience as the mudflats teem with crabs, mudskippers and hermit crabs. You might see a monitor lizard, an otter or the long-tailed macaques feeding on the rich pickings there. When the tide is out, the sandy rock pools are temporary homes for shrimps, crabs, anemones, starfish and fish fry stranded by the receding tide.

Pangolin

With its prehistoric look, the pangolin or scaly anteater is an enigmatic creature, armed with razor sharp scales as a body armour; when threatened it will roll into a scaly ball to protect itself. Its name is derived from the Malay word, *pengguling*, which means 'to roll up'. It is a nocturnal animal – it is only active at night and sleeps in its burrow during the daytime. It has short legs equipped with sharp claws for burrowing into termite mounds and anthills and for climbing. Its extremely elongated thin tongue that can extend to 40cm (16in), coated with sticky saliva, is a useful tool for fishing out termites and ants from their nests. Pangolins live in hollow trunks or underground burrows.

Bako, Kubah and Gunung Gading National Parks

Facilities at Bako National Park

Facilities available at the park include a 24-hour electricity supply at all accommodations, camping sites, day shelters, lockers, public toilets, canteen, education and information centre and video shows. There is a small shop as well as a cafeteria serving simple meals and drinks. Ensure you boil all water before drinking as the water supply is not treated, or else you can buy bottled water from the canteen. There are barbeque pits around the park compound.

To truly appreciate the beauty of the park and to spot its many animals, a trek on one of many trails is worthwhile. There are 16 colour-coded trails in the park, giving a wide range of walking and hiking options to suit all levels of fitness and stamina. The adventurous jungle junkies can opt for overnight camping along the longer trails, like the six-hour hike to Telok Limau, while those who prefer short trails can opt for the Tanjung Sapi Trail, a mere 30-minute trek although it involves a steep climb through cliff vegetation.

The most popular trail in the park is the hour-and-a-half trek to Telok Pandan Kecil and Telok Pandan Besar. This trail traverses forested hills overlooking Telok Assam. The journey goes through scrub vegetation with dwarf trees. The park is a treasure trove of tropical plants, whose variety is astounding and is arguably the richest within any one demarcated area in the state. Watch out for the pitcher plants, the insect-eating plants of Borneo. They are easily seen and there is a wide variety of them all over the park.

Wildlife is scarce in such sparse vegetation though you may spot some birds foraging for grubs and insects on the stunted trees. The path continues along a sandy path before reaching a cliff top revealing a picturesque vista of the secluded bay below and the famous sea stack, the iconic landmark of Bako, just offshore.

A 10-minute descent takes you to one of the best beaches in the park, a white sandy enclave sweeping across the bay and ideal for swimming. Watch out for light-fingered macaque monkeys who prey on unsuspecting bathers and their unattended belongings. Many a time, items of clothing are seen festooned on treetops on the beach like Christmas tree decorations while the simian looters shriek gleefully over their exploits.

A park guide, who will share intimate knowledge of the flora and fauna of the park, is required to accompany visitors on the treks. Unlike lowland forests, the montane and heath forests in Bako are not dense or shaded, so be sure to bring an ample water supply, wear a hat and apply suntan lotion generously to prevent sunstroke and sunburn.

Kubah National Park

Getting There

From Kuching, take a taxi or Petra Jaya bus no. 6 to Kampong Bako (45 minutes). You can charter a boat at the National Park Boat Ticketing Counter (opens daily 08:00–16:15) for the 30-minute sea journey. Alternatively you can book a tour through local travel companies who will arrange for all transfers, accommodation and guides. Contact **Borneo Adventure**: tel: 6082 245 175, e-mail: info@borneoadventure.com It is possible to do a day trip to Bako National Park.

Where To Stay

Bako National Park offers basic accommodation (no air conditioning, but with fans) in forest lodges (rates from RM50 per room), hostels (from RM15 per bed or RM40 per room) and camp sites (RM5 per person). For current rates, reservation and entry fees, contact: **The National Park Booking Office**, Jalan Tun Abang Haji Openg, Kuching, tel: 6082 248 088, e-mail: npbooking@sarawaknet.gov.my

Kubah National Park

One of the richest tropical rainforests in the world lies just 21km (13 miles) from Kuching. The Kubah National Park at the foothills of the Matang range has such a bewildering variety of palms, wild ginger, aroids (jungle yam) and pitcher plant species that botanists are still discovering new species despite the fact that records of plant life have been documented for more than a century.

Gazetted in 1989 and opened to the public in 1995, the 2230ha (5510-acre) park is dominated by a sandstone plateau and three mountains – Gunung Serapi, Gunung Selang and Gunung Sendok. The forest at Kubah National Park is

Kubah National Park

Location: 21km (13 miles) from Kuching.

Size: 2230ha (5510 acres).

Altitude: 911m (2988ft).

Of interest: Palmarium trail, notably *Licuala orbicularis* palm with its decorative round leaves.

Below: The palm forest along the Palmarium trail is one of the richest palm habitats in the world.

Bako, Kubah and Gunung Gading National Parks

mixed dipterocarp, with small areas of scrub forest and isolated patches of *kerangas*, a tropical moist forest. Its rich plant life, proximity to the coastline and varied terrain ensure that Kubah is home to a variety of wildlife, including bearded pigs, more than 50 bird species (including Argus Pheasants and Black Hornbills), sambar deer, mousedeer, civets, porcupines, squirrels and numerous species of amphibians and reptiles. However, most animals in this park are nocturnal and they tend to hide deep in the forest during the day.

Kubah National Park

The park's best-known feature is its palms. Eighty species have been recorded (16 endemic to Sarawak), making Kubah one of the richest palm habitats for its size anywhere in the world. Many of the species were first described by the great Italian botanist Odoardo Beccari (1843–1920), who spent three years in Sarawak (1865–68), recording his findings and experiences in a remarkable book entitled *Wanderings in the Great Forests of Borneo*.

You, however, will not need to wander far. A trek along the Palmarium trail, which starts near the Park Headquarters, will give you a good look at many of the palm species in the park, each clearly labelled. The most noticeable palm is the majestic fan palm (*Licuala orbicularis*) with its almost circular fronds, one of the species endemic to Sarawak. Other plant species found here include a wild ginger (*Hornstedtia piningis*) and a unique-looking aroid species known as Bunga Bangkai in Malay which is endemic to Borneo. Among the many other species of ginger, the *Globba atrosanguines*, with its small bright orange flowers, has a special place in the tradition of the Ibans, the largest ethnic group in Sarawak. It is taboo for the community to walk over the plant and they always make sure they walk around it in their forays into the jungle. The Ibans also forbid anyone to bring the plant to their longhouses but sadly this superstition is not shared by other communities in Sarawak as the plant is a popular house plant and is facing extinction in its natural habitat because of rampant illegal collection. The oldest plant in the park is the prehistoric Chloranthus, *Amorphophallus infundibuliformis*, which is endemic to Sarawak. Like the ginger plant it is also a popular target of illegal collectors. There is also a large variety of ferns in the park and the species that literally stands out from the rest is the tree fern, which grows up to 9m (30ft) high.

Starting at Park Headquarters, visitors can choose different trails to different parts of the park. One of the trails, which begins at the Park Headquarters in Mount Serapi, leads to a telecommunication tower at the summit, offering trekkers a breathtaking view of Kuching (capital of Sarawak), Mount Santubong and the coastline of southwest Sarawak. The peaks of the border range which separates Sarawak from Kalimantan in Indonesia are also seen. The Rayu Trail starts at the 274m (900ft) mark on Mount Serapi

Matang Wildlife Centre

Situated at the western corner of Kubah National Park, lying in the valley of Gunung Serapi, lies Matang Wildlife Centre, located 35km (22 miles) from Kuching. It covers an area of 176ha (435 acres) while Kubah covers 2230ha (5510 acres) and the habitat of both sites is similar to that of Semenggoh. Opened in 1998, the centre was established as a sister facility to Semenggoh Wildlife Centre to conduct orang-utan rehabilitation. It is dedicated to the housing and possible release of animals that have come into conflict with humans via hunting, the pet trade or mistreatment. It is currently home to crocodiles, sun bears, birds, primates, bear cats, leopard cats, porcupines, civets and chelonians. All 11 orang-utans in Matang Wildlife Centre are free-ranging and visitors are allowed to view daily feeding of these orang-utans at the feeding platform.

Bako, Kubah and Gunung Gading National Parks

Semenggoh Wildlife Centre

Feeding time: 09:00–10:00 and 15:00–15:30. Opening times: Mon–Sun (except Fri) 08:00–12:30 and 14:00–16:00; Fri 08:00–11:30 and 14:00–16:00. A permit and a small entrance fee is required to enter Semenggoh Wildlife Centre and this can be obtained at the entrance.

Getting There

Kubah National Park, Matang Wildlife Centre and Semenggoh Wildlife Centre are all in close proximity to the city of Kuching and can be visited as a day trip. You can get there by taxi – a 40-minute drive on a tar road – or through a local travel agent. Kubah National Park is under the protection of the Sarawak Forestry Corporation and visitors can seek assistance from staff stationed at the park. Single entrance fee is RM10 per adult and RM5 for students, senior citizens and the disabled.

and leads to the Matang Wildlife Centre, 2–3 hours away. If you want to take a dip in the cool refreshing mountain water, head for the Waterfall Trail which starts near the 305m (1000ft) mark on Mount Serapi. The trail passes some giant buttress-rooted rainforest trees and a number of *Bintangor* trees, which have been claimed to have properties to cure AIDS – researchers are still working on it. A new trek called the Belian Trail is ideal for mountain jungle trekking beginners. It highlights the conservation of the Belian tree, also known as Borneo Ironwood.

Semenggoh Wildlife Centre

Orang-utans are shy animals and to spot them in the wild may take days, weeks, or even months of trekking. Thankfully, just 33km (20 miles) from Kuching, Semenggoh Wildlife Centre offers the best place to view the enigmatic 'man of the forest'. The wildlife centre is sited in a tropical dipterocarp forest, containing several species of fruiting tree interspersed with patches of *kerangas*, synonymous to the apes' natural habitat in the wild. Set up in 1975, the centre covers an area of 653ha (1616 acres) to rehabilitate confiscated orang-utans into the Semenggoh Forest Reserve. The centre provides veterinary care and carries out captive breeding and research. The centre also houses confiscated animals of other totally protected species, for quarantine and eventual release into other parts of Sarawak.

Throughout the years, the orang-utans at the centre have been successfully adapting to the forest of Semenggoh. The orang-utans used to depend on scheduled feeding times at the centre but now they only come to the centre when food is scarce in the wild, particularly during the low-fruiting season between March and September. Currently, there are 23 orang-utans at Semenggoh Wildlife Centre and all are free-ranging.

Visitors are strictly forbidden to pet, feed or interact with the orang-utans for fear of transmitting diseases to the apes and vice versa and to discourage attachment to humans in order to prepare them to return to the wild. It should be remembered that the orang-utans and all the animals in the centre are wild and predisposed to unpredictable behaviour. Visitors can view daily feeding of orang-utans at the feeding platform.

Gunung Gading National Park

Where To Stay

For those who are prepared to rough it, there is basic accommodation in Kubah National Park and Matang Wildlife Centre in forest lodges, hostels and camp sites. For reservation of accommodation and a park entry permit, contact:

National Park & Wildlife Booking Office,
Sarawak Tourism Complex, Jalan Tun Abang Haji Openg,
tel: 6082 248 088,
fax: 6082 248 087
Online booking: http://ebooking.com.my
e-mail: npbooking@sarawaknet.gov.my

Gunung Gading National Park

Gunung Gading National Park is one of the best and most acessible places to view the Rafflesia's spectacular blooms. Only one species of Rafflesia, R. *tuan-mudae*, is found at the park. Gunung Gading was gazetted as a park in 1983, primarily to provide a conservation zone for the protection of the Rafflesia, but only opened to the public in 1994. The park is about 80km (50 miles) from Kuching by road (1 to 2 hours' drive). To get there you have to pass through the small coastal town of Lundu which is only a five-minute drive from the park. As the Rafflesia has a brief flowering period, visitors to Gunung Gading National Park should enquire beforehand to avoid disappointment. Both the Park Headquarters (tel: 082 735 714) and the National Parks Booking Office in Kuching (tel: 082 248 088) can tell you if a Rafflesia is in full bloom or about to bloom.

Getting There and Accommodation

The Sarawak Transport Company operates buses from Brooke Dockyard at Gambier Road to 3rd Mile bus station and visitors have to continue the journey by taxis to Lundu which will take about 2 hours in total. It is more convenient to take a taxi all the way from Kuching, or contact a tour operator who will arrange transport and a permit. A visit to Gunung Gading is normally a day trip but if visitors wish to stay overnight, there are simple chalet units and hostel accommodation at the park; this has to be booked through the National Park Booking Office in Kuching, tel: (082) 248088, website: http://ebooking.com.my

Gunung Gading National Park

Location: 80km (50 miles) from Kuching.
Size: 4196ha (10,368 acres).
Of interest: Rafflesia viewing.

Bako, Kubah and Gunung Gading National Parks

Above: Rafflesia, the world's largest flower, is one of Gunung Gading's main attractions.

Rafflesia

Besides being credited as the man who founded the island of Singapore, Sir Stamford Raffles was also one of two men from the Western world to discover the world's largest flower. He and Dr Joseph Arnold were the first Europeans to discover the flower in 1818 during a field trip near the town of Bengkulu in Sumatra. That specimen measured 97cm (38in) in diameter and was named *Rafflesia arnoldii* in honour of the two men. However, the flower is now generally referred to as Rafflesia and Sarawak is one of the few places in the world these magnificent blooms are found.

Three species of this holoparasitic (absence of chlorophyll) plants are found in Sarawak: *R. arnoldii*, the biggest among them, *R. pricei* and a species which is endemic to Sarawak, *R. tuan-mudae*. Rafflesia, or *Bunga Pakma* in the Malay language, is a parasitic plant of the gigantic liana vine, *Tetrastigma* of the plant family *Vitaceae*, the only known host of Rafflesia. There are 97 species of *Tetrastigma* in the world and they are found in tropical and

Rafflesia

subtropical Asia. In the regions where Rafflesia occurs, there are at least 57 species of *Tetrastigma*. However, only seven or maybe eight are parasitized by the Rafflesia.

Rafflesias are found only in Southeast Asia, and then only in sub-montane hilly forests at elevations between 400m (1312ft) and 1300m (4265ft). There are thought to be 17 species of Rafflesia, some of which may already be extinct. The Rafflesia is still a mystery and scientists are still unsure why it associates itself with the *Tetrastigma* vine or how the seeds of a Rafflesia germinate and grow. What is known is that threads of tissue spread out within the vine and absorb nutrients. After 18 months a small dark brown bud appears. Such a long period of growth means that there is a high risk of damage; even when a bud forms there is no guarantee that it will mature into a Rafflesia flower. Studies have shown that a high percentage of buds do not survive due to drought or heavy rain. After nine months the brown 'leaves' of the cabbage-like bud open, revealing the underside of the petal-like lobes. It takes several hours for a flower to open fully. There are usually five thick and fleshy red-coloured petals, covered in lighter coloured spots, warts and blotches. The Rafflesia only blooms for three to five days, before it starts to blacken and rot. Rafflesia flowers are either male or female, and therefore cannot self-pollinate. For pollination to occur, a male and a female flower must bloom at the same time and pollen must be transported over considerable distances. Pollination is carried out by carrion flies, so whilst in full bloom the Rafflesia gives off a foul smell of decaying flesh to attract them. Seeds are thought to be dispersed by rodents and other small mammals which eat the flowers.

Like much exotic plant life, Rafflesia cannot escape the threats caused by humankind, particularly loss of habitat. Rafflesia is so specialized, relying as it does on its host, the *Tetrastigma*, that it has a high mortality rate. The establishment of totally protected conservation zones is the only way to preserve this unique gigantic flower. Rare and highly localized in mixed dipterocarp or secondary forest, it can be found at the Gunung Gading National Park, Lanjak-Entimau Wildlife Sanctuary, Padawan near Kuching and the Kelabit Highlands.

Bako, Kubah and Gunung Gading National Parks

Pitcher Plants

There are seven genera of pitcher plants and the largest is the genus Nepenthes (Nepenthaceae) which has its centre of distribution in Borneo. To date, about 80 species of Nepenthes have been discovered and the islands of Borneo and Sumatra host the greatest diversity of these plants, more than anywhere else in the world. In Sarawak, about 20 species of pitcher plants have been discovered and most of them can be found within Sarawak's network of national parks. Mulu National Park boasts 11 species, Kubah National Park has eight species and Bako National Park has six species. Known as periuk kera in Malay, which means 'monkey pot', this plant obtains its nutrients from snacking on insects. It digests them and other organisms in its jug-like trapdoor structures called pitchers. These pitchers are extensions of the leaves of the plant and contain a fluid with digestive enzymes ingeniously designed to lure and trap insects. Some pitchers can catch animals as big as rats. Pitcher plants can grow in a diverse range of habitats and altitudes. Those species which grow from sea level up to 1000m (3281ft) are the lowland species, while highland species grow above 1000m (3281ft). They can be found in peat swamps, heath forests, on limestone cliffs and from mossy forests to sub-alpine vegetation.

Pitcher plants are climbing vines with long stems. Most Nepenthes species can produce two types of pitchers: lower and upper. The lower pitchers usually rest on the ground and are short and rounded in shape. They look different to the

Below: Pitcher plants, locally known as 'monkey pots', are widely found in the national parks of Sarawak, which boasts of 20 species.

Pitcher Plants and Orchids

long, slender upper pitchers which often hang from surrounding vegetation using their climbing stems. The plants can produce pitchers with different colours, sizes and shapes which have spots, blotches, large lips and hair to trap insects. Over-collection in the wild coupled with habitat destruction have put these plants on the endangered list. Therefore, all *Nepenthes* species in Sarawak are protected under the Wildlife Protection Ordinance of 1998 and they have been listed on the Convention on International Trade of Endangered Species (CITES).

Orchids

The smallest orchid species in Sarawak, *Bulbophyllum*, are no more than a few millimeters tall while the tallest among them, the *Vanilla* species, climb up to 30m (98ft) into their host trees. In between there are an estimated 2500 other species, making up to 10% of the total orchid species in the world. Many species have yet to be identified and to date only a total of 499 species from 114 genera, many of which are endemic, have been identified. These botanic jewels are threatened because of their great horticultural value. These include species in the genera of *Arachnis, Phalaenopsis, Renanthera, Rhyncostylis* and *Vanda*. The most outstanding genus is *Paphiopedilum* (slipper orchid), with *P. sanderanium* having appendages up to 50cm (20in) long. There are more than 100 types of slipper orchids growing in the tropical highlands of Malaysia and Borneo. They are classified as endangered species. Some species, such as the white slipper orchid (*Paphiopedilum niveum*), are already in danger of extinction due to over-collection by horticulture enthusiasts.

Orchids are distributed in all forest types throughout Sarawak and they are either epiphytic or terrestrial, although many species are habitat specific, including those that have adapted to the harsh environment of limestone hills. To conserve the species many have been collected for herbarium specimens and *ex-situ* conservation in the Sarawak Forestry's Botanical Research Centre, Semenggoh, near Kuching. Visitors who are game for an orchid trail should head down to any of the national parks in Sarawak where they can spend a few days just exploring the different species. Only wild orchids are protected under the Sarawak Wildlife Ordinance 1998; hybrids are not included.

Pitcher Plant and Wild Orchid Centre

For those who are less adventurous or have a time constraint for jungle trekking, the Pitcher Plant and Wild Orchid Centre, located 16km (10 miles) from Kuching, houses a wide variety of wild orchid species such as *Phalaenopsis violacea*, commonly known as Normah, *Bulbophyllum* spp, *Arundina graminifolia* or Bamboo Orchid, *Coelogyne mayeriana, Dendrobium moschatum, Pomatocalpa kunstleri, Calanthe vestika* and *Phaius tankervilleae*. The 0.4ha (one-acre) centre also has over 30 subspecies of pitcher plants ranging from the common *Nepenthes ampullaria* to hybrids such as *Nepenthes x hookeriana*. The centre is open to the public Tue–Sun, 09:00–17:00.

Bako, Kubah and Gunung Gading National Parks

Sarawak's Orang-utans

Based on a recent survey by Sarawak Forestry, the total population of orang-utans in Sarawak is estimated to be about 2300 individuals and they can be found in three totally protected areas, namely Lanjak Entimau Wildlife Sanctuary, Batang Ai National Park and Ulu Sebuyau National Park, a total area of 250,000ha (617,750 acres). Orang-utans are an endangered species and totally protected by law under the Sarawak Wildlife Protection Ordinance. Severe penalties of a fine between RM25,000 and RM50,000 or two to five years of imprisonment await anyone found in possession of wild plants or animals that are protected. Other primates on this list are the proboscis monkey, banded langur, Hose's langur, Bornean gibbon, silvered langur, white-fronted langur and maroon langur. Orang-utans are also listed under the Convention on International Trade in Endangered Species of Wild Flora and Fauna (CITES).

Orang-utans

The largest tree-dwelling mammal in the world is aptly called orang-utan, which means 'jungle people' or 'man of the forest' in Malay, because they share nearly 97% of the same DNA as humans, making them one of our closest relatives in the animal kingdom. One of the four types of Great Apes, this animal is diurnal (active only during the day), reaching its peaks in the early morning and late afternoon. There are two species, namely *Pongo pygmaeus* of Borneo and the Sumatran species, *Pongo abelii*. In Borneo, orang-utan are further divided into three sub-species, namely *P. pygmaeus* which is found in western Borneo (Sarawak and Kalimantan), *P. wurmbii* which is found in southern Borneo (Kalimantan) and *P. morio* which is found in eastern Borneo (Sabah and Kalimantan).

Bornean orang-utans have interesting orange, brown or maroon, shaggy and coarse long hair. Both male and female orang-utans have throat pouches that allow them to make sounds that resonate through the forest. Their infants are born with pink faces but, as they age, the colour darkens to dark brown. Adult orang-utans weigh between 50kg (110lb) and 100kg (220lb) and measure from 1.25m (4ft) to 1.5m (5ft) in height. Males are twice the size of females. When moving on the ground, the orang-utan walk quadrupedally on their fists, not on their knuckles or bipedally like other great apes. Male orang-utans are easily distinguished by their large size, throat pouch and flanges or cheekpads on either side of the face. The position of their thumbs and big toes gives them the nimbleness to move hand over hand, grasp tree branches in an 'iron fist' manner with their feet and move effortlessly through the rainforest canopy.

The apes build a new nest each night, between 12m (40ft) and 18m (60ft) up the trees, using branches and twigs. But sometimes when there is a shortage of suitable materials or if there is a good food supply located nearby late in the afternoon, the existing nest is re-used. Orang-utans are slow breeders with an inter-birth interval of six to eight years. Females give birth only after reaching maturity at 10 to 15 years of age. The offspring are dependent on their mothers for at least the first five years and, with a life expectancy of 45 years plus, females will normally have no more

Orang-utans

than three births in a lifetime. The female orang-utan's gestation period is eight to nine months, typically giving birth to a single baby and, on rare occasions, twins. Male orang-utans attain full physical and social maturity when they are 13 to 15 years of age.

Orang-utans eat a wide variety of plant species but mainly feed on fruits. They have also been known to fancy buds, flowers, young leaves, bark, sap, vines, orchids, roots and various other plant parts, birds' eggs, spiders, termites, caterpillars, ants, fungi and honey.

Their daily itinerary revolves around feeding, resting and moving between feeding and resting sites. Their daily travel range varies from 90m (98yd) to over 3km (2 miles) with an average of 790m (864yd), although the males generally travel further than the females each day.

Below: A baby orang-utan relaxing at the Semenggoh Wildlife Centre where it is trained for return to the wild.

GUNUNG MULU NATIONAL PARK AND NIAH NATIONAL PARK

Sarawak's national parks offer an exciting range of adventure options, including jungle trekking, river safaris, fishing, camping and caving. Two magnificent cave systems for the budding speleologist are the Mulu Caves in Gunung Mulu National Park and the archeological Niah Cave in Niah National Park. The Mulu Caves are awesome and spectacular and rank among the best natural wonders of the world.

A walk in the forest at night is an eerie experience, with the strange sounds of all the nocturnal creatures and the deafening cacophony of the cicadas and other insects, yet enchanting when fireflies flicker in the dark lighting the way momentarily.

Top Ten

Hornbills
Trogons
Bulbul
Brahminy Kite
Bat Hawk
Monkeys
Sun bears
Civets
Mongoose
Bats

Opposite, top to bottom:
The entrance to the Great Cave at Niah, one of the largest cave chambers in the world; the megabat flying foxes make their nightly foray into the forest in large noisy squadrons, screeching their way into the night to hunt for insects; the famous limestone pinnacles at Gunung Api (Fire Mountain).

Gunung Mulu and Niah National Parks

Gunung Mulu National Park

Gunung Mulu National Park

Location: 100km (62 miles) from Miri. Flight from Kuala Lumpur to Miri is 2 hours 20 minutes.
Size: 544km² (210 sq miles).
Altitude: 2376m (7796ft).
Of interest: Evening exodus of millions of bats leaving Deer Cave, whilst hungry Bat Hawks seek an easy meal.

Situated 100km (62 miles) east of Miri, the oil-rich city in northeastern Sarawak, the Gunung Mulu is the largest national park in the state. It was gazetted in 1974 and spans an area of 544km² (210 sq miles), covering eight different types of forest, including peat swamp, health and mixed dipterocarp, moss forest and stunted upper montane vegetation. Scientific study of the area has been carried out since the 1930s. A joint expedition in the park carried out by the Royal Geographical Society and the Sarawak Government from 1977 to 1982 identified an astounding estimated 3500 species of plants, including 2000 species of flowering plants (several of which were new), 8000 species of fungi and 1700 species of mosses and liverworts. Mulu's fauna is staggeringly impressive, with 20,000 species identified, including 75 species of mammals, 262 species of birds (including the eight species of hornbill found in Sarawak), 75 species of frogs and toads, 47 species of fish, 281 species of butterflies, 52 species of reptiles, 458 species of ants and 20,000 species of invertebrates.

The world's smallest bear, the sun bear, can be found in the park, but is rarely seen. Several species of civet and mongoose are also park residents but, like the sun bear, are difficult to spot. Besides the Bornean squirrels, the most likely animals you will encounter are the monkeys and there are four species to observe: the long-tailed macaque, pig-tailed macaque, Hose's leaf monkey and red leaf monkey.

The park is dominated by three mountains – Gunung Mulu, at 2376m (7796ft) the second highest mountain in Sarawak after Gunung Murud; Gunung Api, at 1750m (5742ft), and Gunung Benarak at 1585m (5200ft). Deep in the heart of these mountains are Sarawak's crown jewels – the Mulu Caves. Visitors to the park are primarily attracted to the four show caves: Deer Cave, Lang Cave, Clearwater Cave and Wind Cave. The massive cave system is one of the largest labyrinths of underground rivers, passages and caves in the world. One of the caves, the Sarawak Chamber, is the largest underground chamber in the world. It is 400m (437yd) wide, 600m (656yd) long and 270m (886ft) high at the highest part of its ceiling – enough room to accommodate St Paul's Cathedral with plenty of room to spare.

Deer Cave

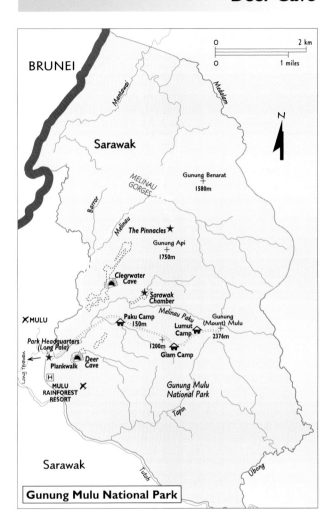

Amorphophallus

Amorphophallus hewittii, a single-leaf plant endemic to Sarawak, produces inflorescence of up to 1.5m tall. The bloom has an unpleasant odour, which attracts insects for its pollination, and lasts only a few days before withering. It grows in rich soils amongst limestone and granite formations. The beautiful, mottled leaf stalks can reach heights of over 3m. The plant flowers only once in its lifetime, then three years after that the leaf withers and dies. This unique plant can be found in the limestone hills and valleys particularly on deep shaded areas of Bau, a former gold-mining town about one hour drive from Kuching, and in the limestone forest of Gunung Mulu National Park.

Deer Cave

The largest of the four show caves in the park, Deer Cave, is an easy trek on a 3km (2-mile) wooden walkway from the Park Headquarters that leads to the entrance. It traverses peat swamp, alluvial flats and limestone outcrops. It is worthwhile pausing along the way to admire the enchanting forest with its array of plants and an ancient Penan burial cave. If you are lucky, you might be able to catch a glimpse of the endangered Rhinoceros

Gunung Mulu and Niah National Parks

A Nightly Exodus

Deer Cave, one of the world's largest, offers a spectacular nightly exodus of the free-tailed bats at dusk. Every night at about six o'clock, except when it rains, millions of these nocturnal creatures fly out of Deer Cave in a continuous stream like a cloud of black smoke in their forage for food. They feed on the thousands of insects that thrive in the forest of the park. They fly in a big convoy, screeching and flapping in a loop pattern to confuse their predators, the bat hawks, which lie in wait every night at the cave entrance ready to swoop down on their prey. The whooshing sound of the bat wings and their screeches can be heard from a great distance. Visitors are treated to a spectacular display of the battle between the bats and bat hawks, with many bats inevitably falling prey to the hawks, enforcing the law of the jungle. To add to the fracas, thousands of swiftlets who share the cave with the bats come home to roost for the night at the same time. It is an experience not to be missed. If you stay for the flight of the bats, be sure to bring along a torchlight because the jungle gets dark very quickly after dusk and the trek back to your accommodation is in total darkness through the forest.

Hornbill in flight, with its noisy wing beat and raucous squawks. Sighting of animals in the forest is very rare as the shy creatures keep well away from the walkway.

Deer Cave was an ancient burial ground for the people who once inhabited the area. Deer used to take shelter in the cave and the local Penan and Berawan tribes named it Deer Cave, or *Gua Payau* in their language. It is reputedly the world's largest cave passage. The vastness of the cave is breathtakingly awesome, measuring 2km (1.2 miles) in length and no less than 90m (295ft) in height at its lowest point. The main chamber near the entrance is 174m (190yd) wide and 122m (400ft) high and features a curious rock formation that uncannily resembles the profile of Abraham Lincoln silhouetted against the sunlight when viewed from inside the cave. A narrow concrete path is built over the guano-filled cave floor to enable visitors to explore deeper into the cave. Although the path is dimly lit, it is advisable to bring a strong torchlight to navigate the damp and dark passage, which smells of ammonia emanating from the knee-deep guano. Further in the cave among boulders and rocks is another notable feature of the cave: the 'Adam and Eve Shower', a cascade of water gushing through a hollow stalactite 120m (394ft) high. It is near the 'Garden of Eden', where the cave roof has partially collapsed, creating a sunlit clearing with lush vegetation and a stream, before the passage continues deep into the mountain. The cave is home to millions of free-tailed bats along with thousands of swiftlets usually found near the entrances of the caves, and a host of insects including earwigs, cicadas and centipedes.

Lang's Cave

A visit to this stunning cave is best combined with Deer Cave as they are next to each other. Named after the guide who introduced it to speleologists in 1977, this cave is a few minutes' walk from Deer Cave. It is one of the smaller caves in Mulu but arguably the most beautiful, with its wonderful array of stalactites, stalagmites and helictites (slender calcium carbonate formations on the floor, wall and ceiling). Some of these formations are within touching distance from the walkways, but visitors are requested not to touch them. The compact chamber is lit to reveal the spectacular beauty of the golden rock formations.

Wind Cave and Clearwater Cave

You can spot some of the cave denizens like the small colony of bats, swiftlets, spiders and, sometimes, even snakes. It is the smallest but most attractive of all the show caves.

Wind Cave

Approachable only by the Melinau River, a wooden walkway from its bank leads along the steep limestone cliff above the river and down a gentle slope to the cave entrance. This cave is part of the Clearwater Cave system and is usually visited as part of an excursion there. At the entrance you will feel a cool draught coming out from the cave, a phenomenon that gives the cave its name. The walkway leads into the cave under a shaft, through which daylight penetrates the chamber, and ends up in the King's Room. Aptly named because of its magnificent stalactites and stalagmites, the rock formation is said to resemble a king seated on a throne with his courtiers in attendance. This enchanting cave is truly spectacular. One of the entrances to the cave is a burial site estimated to be between 1500 and 3000 years old and, of course, reputedly haunted.

Clearwater Cave

The passage in Clearwater Cave is the longest in Southeast Asia and to date only a 107km (66-mile) section of the passage has been surveyed. The cave can be reached via a 4km (2.5-mile) nature trail entailing a two-hour walk or a half-hour boat ride on the Melinau River (depending on the water level). Alternatively, from Wind Cave you can either follow a plankwalk or take a boat to a picnic area near the entrance of Clearwater Cave. Either way the journey takes about 5 minutes up a flight of 200 steps leading through the forest to the mouth of Clearwater Cave. With its underground river, Clearwater is a fascinating cave to stroll around. Plankwalks, paths and small floating bridges make this an easy and enjoyable experience. Watch out for the rare one-leafed plants of *Monophyllaea* at the cave entrance, where you can also see beautiful dropstone formations and tall stalagmites rising from its floor. A crystal clear pool, filled by water that flows out of the cave, provides an excellent swimming and picnic area at the bottom of the steps, a cool and refreshing break after a hectic tour of the cave. There are picnic benches where you can relax and admire the tranquil beauty of the rainforest or to marvel at

The Berawans

The Berawans are an indigenous tribe who belong to the Orang Ulu sub-group, the 'people of the interior', and their population numbers fewer than 5000 in Sarawak. They live on their ancestral lands along the Melinau River in Mulu National Park and in Loagan Bunut National Park around Lake Bunut. They are skilled hunter-gatherers and live off the land. They also fish from the lake, using the age-old method called *selambau* to harvest fish when the waters recede during the dry season. Because of their ancestry, they are given special rights in the national parks to fish, cut trees to build their houses, and collect produce from the forest. With the advent of tourism, they have benefited from the industry by becoming nature guides, with their intimate knowledge of the area, while some operate rustic chalets as accommodation for visitors. The Berawans are excellent hosts and welcome visitors to their longhouses. They are also skilled musicians, playing instruments fashioned out of bamboo and wood, and they are famous for their *sapeh* music – a kind of native guitar that plays mesmerizing tunes.

Gunung Mulu and Niah National Parks

Head-hunter's Trail

For the adventurous who are physically fit, the Head-hunter's Trail is a challenging and amazing way to experience a rainforest and riverine expedition in the Mulu National Park area. The trail traces the ancient route taken by head-hunting parties of the Kayan tribe when they used to travel up the Melinau River to the Melinau Gorge, after which they dragged their boats overland for 3km (1.9 miles) until they reached the banks of the Terikan River. From there, they sailed up the river to launch their head-hunting raids against rival tribes in the Limbang area. Today, visitors can embark on the same trail on a more peaceful mission – to visit the longhouse at Rumah Bala Lesong for an overnight stay before continuing downriver to Nanga Medamit, another native settlement. From here it is possible to travel by road to Limbang, and thence to Miri. Tour operators can offer this tour in conjunction with the Pinnacles climb on a five-day/four-night package. Contact Borneo Adventure for details.

the delicate butterflies, usually of the Common Bluebottle species that are often found fluttering in swarms around the river bank. If you are lucky you may even see the Rajah Brooke butterfly with its huge bright green coloured wings.

Adventure Caving

For those who want to explore Mulu caves off-trail, the National Park Department has identified a number of caves that are deemed suitable for adventure caving. Adventure caving is awesome and challenging and is recommended only for experienced speleologists and those who are fit. An expedition at these caves often involves wading across rivers or streams, squeezing in between rocks and crevices, crawling along low passages, swimming through underground rivers and getting covered in mud. Some of Mulu's caving trips require knowledge of technical rope work like 'single rope technique' (SRT), as abseiling and climbing are involved.

Most adventure caving expeditions are full-day trips, and some might involve overnight stays at jungle camps. Adventure caving trips can be arranged at the Park Headquarters or by tour companies who operate Mulu packages. Although some of the more popular caves have been equipped with fixed ropes on short descents, climbs and traverses, rigging equipment, SRT and climbing ropes are useful. The Park Headquarters does not provide extensive caving equipment and anyone planning to do a series of adventure caving trips is advised to bring their own equipment. To date, the locations for adventure caving include: Benarat Caverns; Clearwater/Snake Track; Cobra; Cobweb; Deer Water; Drunken Forest; Lagang; Link/Clearwater; Monkey; Nasib Bagus and Sarawak Chamber; Porcupine; Snake and Wind Caves.

The Limestone Pinnacles of Gunung Api (Fire Mountain)

The famous Pinnacles at Mulu are a magnificent natural phenomenon, a sight to behold, especially from the air when flying to Mulu from Miri or vice versa. On a clear day when the weather is fine, the pilot of the Twin-Otter aircraft will fly over the Pinnacle affording a panoramic view of the razor-sharp cluster

Gunung Api

of limestone rock formations that sprout from the lush forest, towering 45m (148ft) into the air, mid-way up the slopes of Gunung Api. The majestic ash-white blades stand like sentinels over the mountainous expanse. On *terra firma* the pinnacle is best viewed from a point 1000m (3281ft) up Gunung Api. This involves an expedition, the Pinnacle Summit Trek, lasting 3 days and 2 nights and should only be undertaken by those who are physically fit with boundless stamina. Spenser St John, who made the first attempt to climb Gunung Mulu in 1856, described the Pinnacles as 'the world's most nightmarish surface to travel over'. The rocks are really sharp and you should wear gloves and strong boots to avoid cutting yourself. The first stage is a 1–2 hour boat trip, depending on the water level, along the Melinau River to Kuala Barror. A relatively easy trail of 7.8km (5 miles) leads to Base Camp 5 from Kuala Berar, following flat jungle terrain and taking 2–3 hours. Camp 5 is near the Melinau Gorge which separates Gunung Benarat from Gunung Api. There is hostel-style accommodation at the camp and cooking facilities. The Melinau River in front of Camp 5 is crystal clear and ideal for a swim after the trek.

Below: *Many species of orchids, some rare, are found on the montane forest slopes of Gunung Mulu.*

The Pinnacle Summit Trek starts at daybreak on the 2.4km (1.5-mile) trail which rises some 1200m (3937ft) from Camp 5 to the viewpoint, passing through lowland dipterocarp forest before climbing steeply through moss forest. It takes about four hours to reach the viewing point and the final section of the trail is near vertical, with rope sections and 15 aluminium ladders strategically positioned to help with the climb. The vegetation is sparse although orchids, rhododendrons and pitcher plants thrive in the area, and can be seen along the trail. There is not much time to linger as the climbers must reach base camp before sundown. The breathtaking panoramic view of the Pinnacles is well worth the effort for those who are brave and strong enough to undertake this adventure.

Gunung Mulu and Niah National Parks

Getting there

Miri serves as the main gateway to Gunung Mulu National Park. Malaysian Airlines operates scheduled services from Miri and Limbang to Mulu using 19-seater Twin Otter aircrafts. The flight takes approximately 45 minutes. The national park can also be reached by boat up the Baram River but this requires prior arrangement with travel agencies as there is no regular service via this route.

Accommodation

There are several chalets, a rest house and a hostel at the Park Headquarters. The rooms are spartan but comfortable and reasonably priced, and there are cooking facilities to prepare simple meals. There are also public toilets, washrooms, a canteen and an information centre at the Park Headquarters. Permits and bookings for these rooms can be made at the National Parks and Wildlife Centre at 452 Jalan Melayu in Miri, tel: 6085 434 180, website: http://ebooking.com.my

There are also several lodges and rest houses, run privately by tour operators. A five-star hotel, The Royal Mulu Resort, situated along the Melinau River, is adjacent to the park. These facilities can be booked through local travel companies such as Borneo Adventure, Miri, tel : 6085 424 332, www.borneoadventure.com and Tropical Adventure, Miri, tel: 6085 419 337.

Niah National Park

This national park is best known for its giant cave complex, which is rated the most important archaeological site in Southeast Asia. Archaeologists have uncovered remains of prehistoric man dating back at least 30,000 years, and unique cave paintings and boat-shaped coffins were found in one of the caves.

Niah National Park

Location: 80km (50 miles) from Miri.
Size: 3140ha (7759 acres).
Of interest: Cave exploration in designated caves, jungle trekking and bird-watching.

The caves were declared a National Historic Monument in 1958 but Niah National Park, which covers 3140ha (7759 acres) of forests around the caves, was only gazetted in 1974. Such is the archaeological importance of Niah caves that UNESCO's World Heritage committee has proposed the park be recognized as a World Heritage Site. The archaeological importance of the caves overshadows the richness of the flora and fauna of the park.

Niah National Park

Bird-watching

The park is an excellent bird-watching site and bird life includes the Oriental Pied Hornbill, which prefers open habitat such as forest edges and secondary forest, making them easy to spot. They often form noisy parties of more than 20 individuals, flapping and gliding from tree to tree as they feed on fruits, lizards and insects. Leafbirds, identified by their overall green colour with black or blue markings, are often spotted near the banks of the Subis River and other streams running through the park. They eat mainly fruits and build cup-shaped nests on the leafy ends of branches. Other birds commonly spotted in the same area are trogons, drongos and malcohas. A common bird easily spotted in the park are the bulbuls, which form large families that forage for fruits and insects near river banks and forest edges. These birds have rather short wings and longish bills and are mostly brownish in colour, some with an erectile crest. Bat Hawks, Brahminy Kites and Eagle Owls may also be spotted, especially near the caves as they feed on the thousands of bats and swiftlets found there.

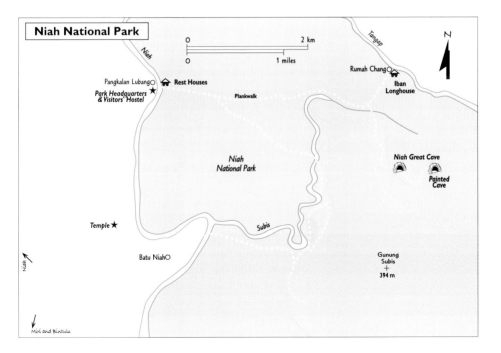

Gunung Mulu and Niah National Parks

Four major forest types are found in Niah National Park – riverine forest and mixed dipterocarp in low ground, limestone forest among the limestone hills which cover more than half of the park, and secondary forest in various stages of regeneration in abandoned areas of shifting cultivation. The diversity of habitats allows for a great variety of plant life which is also found all over the state. You should look out for fungi, easily spotted in the park. The fruitbodies (the visible upper part) of the fungi are attractive and colourful. The common species are coral fungi, earth stars, stinkhorns, birds' nest fungi, pore fungi and cup fungi, all easily spotted growing on dead plant materials like leaves, logs, branches and twigs. Fungi are important sources of food for animals and insects in the forests.

These predators can be seen hovering above the entrances of caves, especially around dusk, waiting for their prey to exit.

Nature's Bounty

Among the locals, the Niah Caves are better known for their bats and swiftlets because they have been and still are a lucrative business source for people living in the area. The swiftlet nests are edible and are a highly prized health food among Chinese people. A kilogram of good quality birds' nest can fetch more than RM12,000 in the market. Sadly the high prices of the swiftlets' nests are the cause of their alarming decline. Estimates recorded between 1935 and 1958 put the number of birds in caves at between 1.5 million and 1.7 million but, despite regulations and restrictions on nest collecting, over-collecting and poaching have caused the population to fall to an alarming estimate of 150,000 birds. Now nest collecting is strictly controlled and only licensed collectors can carry out this trade twice a year: from May to June and from October to November.

Nest collection is one of the main attractions of the park as this trade is spectacular and hazardous. Collectors risk life and limb climbing up long belian (ironwood) poles that hang from the roof of the caves. There are five species of swiftlets in Borneo and they differ very little in size and colour. They are mostly dark grey-brown or black with white patches on their underparts or base of their tails and their wing length varies from 10cm (4in) to 16cm (6in). Not all the swiftlets' nests are edible and the species of edible-nest swiftlet (*Collocalia fuciphaga*) that make the highest quality nest are not found in the Niah Caves. The main swiftlet species of the caves is the Black-nest Swiftlet (*C. maxima*) but their nests are of inferior quality. All swiftlets make their nests by using their glutinous saliva as cement to affix their own feathers which form the bulk of the nests as in the case of the Black-nest Swiftlet. But the use of vegetable matter such as moss, ferns and liverworts used by the Mossy-nest Swiftlet (*C. salagana*) renders their nests valueless. The edible part of the nests is the jelly-like saliva that cements the nests. Preparing them for market entails the tedious work of soaking them and picking out the feathers. The quality of the nests is determined by the lack of impurities in the nests.

Trails

Bats provide a humbler business opportunity. Guano (droppings that pile up on the floors of caves) is a good natural fertilizer and it used to be collected and sold to farmers by the sackful. However, with the growing preference for chemical fertilizers among farmers, guano collection is well past its demand.

There are six species of bats that roost in the caves. A 1958 count of bats estimated there were about 300,000 of them in the caves but a recent census indicated a substantial reduction in the population. Naturally they occupy the darker parts of the cave, with the nectar bats and naked bats occupying the high roofs of the main chambers in tight colonies making an incessant cacophony of chattering screeches and calls. The lesser bent-winged bats roost in clusters in dark tunnels and grottos, while the Cantor's and Diadem roundleaf bats roost singly. The birds and the bats co-exist peacefully in their own roosts close to each other. This is possible because they seldom get in one another's way as the birds fly out in the day time to feed while the bats sleep, and the bats feed at night while the birds roost – a convenient schedule for co-existence.

Trails

The park has an excellent trail system, ranging from comfortable plank walkways (heading out from the Park Headquarters to the caves) to more strenuous hikes up limestone hills. Torch lights are essential for cave visits, and make sure you wear sturdy hiking shoes with good traction as the trails in the caves can be slippery and muddy especially when it rains.

Great Cave Trail

This is an easy 4km (2.5-mile) walk from Park Headquarters to the entrance of the Great Cave, which takes about 90 minutes at a leisurely pace. The mistake most visitors make is to hurry to the caves, thereby missing the beauty of the forest they are passing through. Keep a sharp eye out for fungi on the forest floor and fallen tree trunks – they are worth stopping for. Sit quietly for a while along the walkway and you will be rewarded with the sounds of the forest as birds and small animals, reassured by your silence and stillness, will come out of their hiding places and

Fauna in Niah

There are 64 species of mammals, 25 of which are bats, in the park besides 190 species of birds, 48 snakes, 24 fish and 22 frogs. The most commonly spotted animals in the park are the long-tailed macaques which forage in groups for fruits, seeds and leaves, and small animals such as the Plain Pygmy squirrel which measure only 12cm (5in) from head to tail and can be seen scurrying up tree trunks and along branches. Most of the other animals in the park are hard to spot as the large numbers of visitors have caused them to retreat deep into the forest. Yet calls of barking deer, sambar deer, bearded pig and gibbons are often heard in the remote areas of the park. Nocturnal animals like civets are often seen near the Park Headquarters at night. Excavations in the caves have unearthed prehistoric skeletons of giant wild pigs, anteaters and tapir, now extinct in Borneo, while as recently as 1958 the wild ox had been spotted in the area before it followed the Sumatran rhinoceros, orang-utan and clouded leopard into extinction in Niah National Park.

Gunung Mulu and Niah National Parks

Above: *Long-tailed macaques are commonly found in the park, moving in large noisy groups foraging for food.*

resume their chatterings and food gathering. Among the first to reappear near the plank walkway are usually the lizards, squirrels and long-tailed macaques. Butterflies, dragonflies and electric blue damselflies are particularly numerous.

Steps have been built at steep sections of the trail leading to the West Mouth, the main entrance to the Great Cave. Here you can see belian (Bornean ironwood) poles, joined in lengths up to 45m (148ft) long, hanging from the ceiling, some installed more than 80 years ago to enable collectors to reach the birds' nests. Some 100m (358ft) inside the cave are the prehistoric excavation sites that give the caves their world fame. The cave is among the largest in the world, the main chamber being 60m (197ft) high and 90m (295ft) wide. The high-pitched calls of the swiftlets, the fluttering of their wings and the echoes of the noises made by nest collectors in the semi-darkness broken only by shafts of sunlight streaming through holes in the roof, coupled with the sense that you are at an important prehistoric site, give the caves a surreal atmosphere.

Painted Cave
A 600m (1968ft) trail through a valley between two limestone hills leads from the Great Cave to the smaller Painted Cave. This is where the prehistoric cave paintings and canoe-shaped coffins are found. The paintings and coffins are fenced off to prevent visitors getting too near and causing any damage.

Madu Trail
Another trail in the park is the Jalan Madu Trail that follows the base of a limestone cliff along Gunung Subis. You cross a bridge that spans the Subis River along the trail and it is a good spot for bird-watching. It is not advisable to hike this trail during wet weather as it is muddy and gets flooded at certain parts after a heavy downpour.

Getting There and Accommodation

Bukit Kasut Trail

The Bukit Kasut Trail leads up the 205m (673ft) limestone hill overlooking Niah town and the coastal plain in the distance. Proper hiking shoes are essential for this climb as it is steep and strenuous. Dipterocarp trees grow on the hill; their seeds have two large transparent wings enabling the wind to carry them for great distances.

Rumah Chang

Rumah Chang, an Iban longhouse, is located just outside the perimeter of the park. The trail branches from the main wooden walkway not far from the Park Headquarters and it takes only a 20-minute walk to reach the longhouse. Here you can buy Iban handicrafts and see life in a longhouse.

Getting There

The Niah National Park lies off the Miri-Bintulu highway about two hours' drive from Miri and three hours from Bintulu. There are regular bus services from Bintulu and Miri to Batu Niah, a small town near the park. Visitors can also charter taxis that will take them right to the Park Headquarters.

Bookings for accommodation and permits can be made through the National Parks Wildlife office in Miri, tel: 6085 436 637 (the same procedure as accommodation/permits for Mulu).

Accommodation

There are several hostels, chalets and lodges in the park. There are 10 rooms with four beds per room in each hostel, while the Jungle Lodge has two rooms with two beds in each. The lodgings are provided with electricity, showers, cooking facilities and refrigerators.

There are also camping sites for up to 300 campers. Local travel companies offer package tours to the park (see travel companies for Mulu, page 84).

Other facilities

These include public toilets and washrooms, a canteen and an information centre.

BATANG AI NATIONAL PARK AND LANJAK ENTIMAU WILDLIFE SANCTUARY

Batang Ai National Park adjoins the Lanjak Entimau Wildlife Sanctuary and together they form the largest trans-boundary protected forest area in the tropics, merging into Bentuan–Karimun National Park in Indonesia. The parks and the sanctuary cover a combined area of 10,000km² (3860 sq miles) of hilly forests stretching 200km (124 miles) along the Malaysia/Indonesia border right in the heart of Borneo. Lanjak Entimau Wildlife Sanctuary and Batang Ai National Park are home to the only viable population of orang-utan in Sarawak. It is estimated that the world population of orang-utan in the wild is 20,000 to 27,000, with about 20,000 in Borneo and the rest in Sumatra.

Lanjak-Entimau Wildlife Sanctuary, established in 1983, is a Totally Protected Area (TPA) covering 1688km² (652 sq miles) of forested hills. It is open only for scientists with research permits because various conservation and management projects funded by the International Tropical Timber Organization (ITTO) are located in it. While the scientific research and study is being undertaken, it is strictly off limits to visitors.

Top Ten

Hornbills
Great Argus Pheasant
Bulwer's Pheasant
Crested Partridge
Babblers
Orang-utan
Gibbons
White-fronted langur
Bearded pig
Sun bear

Opposite, top to bottom: This longhouse-style building at the Hilton Batang Ai Resort offers luxury accommodation amid the rainforest; the stunningly beautiful scenery of the Batang Ai Lake viewed from the Batang Ai Resort; narrow longboats are the only means of transport to the Iban longhouses upriver.

Batang Ai NP & Lanjak Entimau Wildlife Sanctuary

Batang Ai National Park

Longhouses of Sarawak

A visit to Batang Ai National Park is not complete without a visit to a longhouse. Highly recommended is a three day two night trip to Nanga Sumpa Longhouse of the Iban tribe in Ulu Ai, a two-hour boat ride up the Batang Ai River from the jetty. Tourists are accommodated at the Borneo Adventure Visitors' Lodge adjacent to Nanga Sumpa Longhouse. The Ibans are very hospitable people and they welcome visitors to join in their evening meal, the drinking of home-brewed rice wine called *tuak* and sometimes traditional dancing. Borneo Adventure contributes a percentage of their revenue to the longhouse for their upkeep and to help in the educational needs of the children. For trips to Nanga Sumpa, contact Borneo Adventure in Kuching, www.borneoadventure.com

Only the 270km^2 (104 sq mile) Batang Ai National Park, gazetted in 1991, is open for visitors and in many ways it's a scaled-down version of Lanjak Entimau as they share similar habitats and fauna. The park encompasses the tributaries and headwaters of the Batang Ai River which flows into the reservoir of the Batang Ai hydroelectric dam operated by Sarawak Electricity Corporation. The establishment of the park fulfilled the dual purpose of conserving wildlife and protecting the watershed as logging in the forests would have rapidly resulted in the silting-up of the reservoir. Prior to the establishment of the park and the building of the dam, the area was inhabited by the Ibans (the largest ethnic group in Sarawak). They were allowed to remain in the area within the boundary of the park while those who were displaced by the reservoir were permitted to move up-river, making Batang Ai National Park unusual in that people live in it. To balance conservation and the needs of the local community, a co-operative (Koperasi Serbaguna Batang Ai) was set up to involve them in the management of the park. They derive income from operating boat services and providing accommodation for visitors to the park. They also sell handicrafts to tourists, while some work as guides, park rangers and game wardens in the national park and the Lanjak Entimau Wildlife Sanctuary. In return, they confine their farming to previously cultivated areas outside the park and limit their hunting and gathering of jungle produce. They can fell timber for their own use but commercial logging is strictly forbidden. The Ibans live in longhouses and visitors to the park can visit their community either on day-trips or stay overnight to experience their traditional lifestyle.

Longhouses of Sarawak

The longhouse is the traditional dwelling of the Iban, Bidayuh and Orang Ulu peoples. It is the oldest form of architecture in the country. The longhouse is built in linear fashion under one roof and has a communal hallway and verandah, but separate apartments for each family, sometimes numbering 80 families. There is usually one main exit and fearsome faces or protection motifs (as in Orang Ulu tribes of Kayan and Kenyah longhouses) are carved on the door to frighten evil spirits away. The construction of a longhouse involves strict ritual, with sacrifice and offerings to the

Batang Ai National Park

earth spirits. The site chosen is usually by a river for water supply, fishing and transport or on high ground for defense purposes. Each longhouse is ruled by a chieftain or *tuai rumah* who presides over social and judicial matters. Old war trophies of human skulls, reminders of the savage days of head-hunting, hang in clusters over the rafters in the gallery in order to ward off evil spirits.

Fauna
The main attraction of Batang Ai National Park is the excellent chance of sighting orang-utans in the wild (and also the emblematic hornbills). The park has many mammals of which the star is the orang-utan. As it is taboo for the Ibans to hunt orang-utans, they are less wary of people and venture closer to human settlements than other big animals in the park. Other primates in the park are the Bornean gibbons whose melancholic calls can quite often be heard in the forest. These territory-marking calls can be heard up to 2km (1.25 miles) away. They travel in small groups, usually comprising a male and female couple and one to three of their offspring of different ages. Only one baby is born at a time and they take seven to eight years to reach maturity and separate

Batang Ai National Park

Location: 275km (171 miles) from Kuching.
Size: 270km² (104 sq miles).
Of interest: Nature walks, jungle trekking and a visit to the Iban longhouses.

Batang Ai NP & Lanjak Entimau Wildlife Sanctuary

from the family. Gibbons feed mainly on fruits and leaves and sometimes flowers and insects. They use their long arms to swing from branch to branch and can reach amazing speeds. The gibbons in Batang Ai and Lanjak Entimau are basically grey-brown in colour with tufts of black on their underparts and heads. It is estimated that there are about 24,000 gibbons in Batang Ai and Lanjak Entimau, the largest remaining population of this primate in Sarawak. They are mostly spotted in the isolated southern part of the park as hunting in the past had caused them to fear humans.

Below: *The slow loris, a nocturnal and arboreal primate, is often spotted on night safari, perched high in a tree with a pair of red eyes peering from the darkness.*

The white-fronted langur is also found in the park and sanctuary, although not much is known about them aside from the fact that their habits are similar to other langurs and leaf monkeys. This species is endemic to Borneo and is confined to hill forests in the centre of the island. Hunting them for their meat and bezoar stones in their stomachs – used in Chinese traditional medicine – has pushed this animal to the edge of extinction. The maroon or red langur also inhabits the park and sanctuary. Like their white-fronted cousins they feed on young leaves, seeds, fruits and flowers and move in small groups. Once this species of langur occurred in most of the Bornean lowlands but hunting drove them to extinction, pushing the remainder of the dwindling population deep into the hill forests of central Borneo.

Batang Ai National Park

The bearded pigs, barking deer and sambar deer found in the park are difficult to spot due to the dense vegetation and their wariness of human presence. They are often hunted for their meat. The best places to observe the animals are at salt licks but even then they will retreat deep into the forest at the mere hint of human presence.

The smaller animals like squirrels are easier to sight and there is a bewildering variety of squirrels in the park. Among the larger ones are the giant squirrel, which measures up to 35cm (14in), the horse-tailed squirrel and the prevost squirrel, a species that is found only in the heart of Borneo. Another of the large squirrels is the tufted ground squirrel which is as big as the giant squirrel but is rarely seen and seems only to occur in small numbers in the park. Nine other species of smaller squirrels have been recorded in the park and there could be others not yet seen closely enough to be identified.

The common porcupine and long-tailed porcupine also dwell in Batang Ai National Park but are seldom seen except for occasional sightings of their loose spines on the forest floor. These burrowing animals are caught by locals by placing traps at the entrances of their burrows and then smoking them out.

Torn-open hollow tree trunks are signs of the sun bear's presence in the park after they have raided bee hives for honey. These bears are occasionally seen in the forest but they are rare. Two nocturnal primates found in the park are the western tarsier and the slow loris. These are very small animals and the tarsier could easily sit in the palm of a person's hand while the slow loris is only slightly bigger. These animals feed mainly on insects and are specially adapted to moving among small trees, the tarsier leaping from sapling to sapling and the slow loris, as its name implies, creeping in slow motion, catching insects through stealth rather than speed as in the case of the tarsier. Their large eyes evolved from their need to see in the dark and this, combined with their small furry bodies, have led to comparisons with 'ET', the alien in the movie. The tarsier, known locally as *kerak hantu* (meaning 'ghost monkey'), can turn its head 180 degrees, giving it the ability to see directly behind itself. These attributes and their

Hilton Batang Ai Longhouse Resort

Nestled by the bank of the picturesque Batang Ai Lake with the rainforest as its backdrop, the resort offers an exotic location to explore the jungle in style and comfort. Built in the style of a traditional longhouse, the rooms are all furnished to a high standard (with air conditioning) and decorated in a traditional native Borneo decor. It is a great base for going on a wildlife expedition and for jungle trekking or embarking on a day trip to authentic Iban longhouses nearby. After a day's adventure, the pool offers an idyllic place to cool down and relax, with the jungle right on the doorstep, emanating the sounds and sights of nature. Watch out for hornbills flying by, or the beautiful giant atlas moths.

Batang Ai NP & Lanjak Entimau Wildlife Sanctuary

Paws For Thought

The feline fauna in Batang Ai includes the Malay civet and the masked palm civet but the most magnificent among the animals in the area is the elusive clouded leopard. It is known to possess the longest and strongest teeth in relation to its size and the longest tail of all the world's cat species. Measuring 1.5m (5ft) from nose to tail, it is the largest of Borneo's cats and can jump 4.5m (15ft) or more from branch to branch. Its coat varies from pale sandy brown to rich yellowish or very dark brown with cloud-like markings on the sides of its body, hence its name. Occupying the top of the food chain in the forest, it is active mainly at night but can also hunt during the day. Pigs, deer, monkeys and sometimes even orang-utans are prey to this deadly predator. Its beautiful fur and long teeth are contributory factors for its being hunted to the brink of extinction as the leopard's pelt is used to make a warrior's vest among the local people and the teeth for necklaces. Once found all over Borneo, the clouded leopard is now extinct in the lowland forests due to over-hunting, depletion of forest cover and lack of prey animals. Now they are almost exclusively found in the deep forests of national parks and wildlife sanctuaries and the chance of sighting them is slim.

pint size put them off the hunters' list resulting in them being easily found near human settlements, although you are more likely to see only the glow of their large eyes in trees at night.

There are a few carnivores, including the smallest of five species of otters in Borneo, the Oriental small-clawed otter. You can catch glimpses of them gambolling in groups in the river looking for small fish and crabs. They are brown or greyish brown in colour with buffy patches covering their neck, chin, cheeks and throat. The yellow-throated marten is often sighted. Walking or jumping, they are almost always in pairs, with their tails held up, hunting for small animals on the forest floor and in the canopy.

Birds

Seven of the eight species of hornbills are found in the Lanjak Entimau/Batang Ai area, five of which have been recorded in the national park. The species that stands literally head and shoulder above others is the Rhinoceros Hornbill, which at 90cm (3ft) in length is among the largest birds in the forest. Cloaked in black features with a white-feathered abdomen and an enormous beak topped by an orange casque, they fly in groups of up to 25 non-breeding adults, emitting loud braying calls as they search for the fruits which form the bulk of their diet. They also feed on insects, tree frogs and lizards. They are the bullies among other fruit-eating birds, often arriving late at fruiting trees but frightening off earlier arrivals with aggressive displays of head jerking, lifting their bills upwards with each cantankerous call while bouncing the branches on which the other birds perch. These intimidating movements are adapted by the Ibans in their traditional warrior dances, the *ngajat*. This species was chosen as the state emblem of Sarawak, hence the state is sometimes known as *Bumi Kenyalang* (Land of the Hornbill).

Among the Ibans, the hornbill is revered as the messenger between this world and the spiritual world. Sadly their lofty status has not protected them from hunters and their loud calls often betray their movements to poachers, who sell their decorative feathers and casques for a high price. The other hornbill species sighted in Batang Ai is the Helmeted Hornbill, the largest among the hornbills, measuring 120cm (4ft). These birds usually move

Birds

about in pairs and sometimes in small groups of up to eight. They are also poached for their large casques that are used as 'hornbill ivory' for carving and for their supposed medicinal properties. The Bushy-crested Hornbills are commonly found in Batang Ai and, like the other hornbills, they usually move about in raucous groups. These are territorial birds and a group of about five adults will occupy an area of about 6km² (2.3 sq miles) depending on the abundance of wild fruit trees. Two other species, which are territorial, are the White-crested Hornbill and the Black Hornbill. They are sometimes sighted among tall trees, especially near river banks.

Ground birds include the Great Argus Pheasant, Bulwer's Pheasant, Crestless Fireback and Crested Patridge. Canopy-dwelling birds are more often heard than seen and these include 15 species of bulbuls, barbets, woodpeckers, babblers (17 species have been recorded in the park), shamas, flycatchers,

Below: The Rhinoceros Hornbill is a magnificent bird, blessed with striking black and white tail feathers and an enormous bill topped by an orange casque. It is among the largest of forest birds.

Batang Ai NP & Lanjak Entimau Wildlife Sanctuary

Plant Life

As parts of the park have been inhabited by the Ibans for hundreds of years, the area has a unique mix of vegetation types. The park primarily comprises lowland mixed dipterocarp forest and, at 500m (1641ft) and above, hill mixed dipterocarp. In areas that had been farmed before, especially near the southern edge, there is an old secondary forest and active shifting cultivation areas that are dotted with burial grounds. Batang Ai National Park has a remarkable biodiversity, with over 1000 tree species, while 200 herbs, shrubs and climbers have been recorded there and its surrounding forests. The Ibans living in this area gather 140 different kinds of medicinal plants, eat 14 kinds of wild fruits and 36 kinds of jungle vegetable. Forest trees and plants are also important as a source of wood, fibre, rattan, bamboo and aromatic resins for the local people.

fantails, flowerpeckers, sunbirds, bristleheads, spidercatchers, trogons, drongos, tree swiftlets, several species of cuckoos and the rare Malaysian Honey Guide. The Ibans have a close spiritual affinity with birds and regard two species of kingfishers as omen birds and the Brahminy Kite as the embodiment of *Singalang Burung*, their god of war.

Other vertebrates found in the park and its adjoining forests include 13 snake species, 13 lizard species, two types of river turtles, spiny hill turtles, an astonishing 52 species of frogs, two burrowing legless amphibians and over 80 fish species. There is an incredible variety of insects and other invertebrates, many of which have yet to be recorded.

Treks and Trails

The five trails in the park showcase every aspect of the park's terrain and vegetation and you will come across ancient burial grounds scattered around the area. Visitors must be accompanied by registered guides at all times. All trails end at a pick-up point for longboat transport back to Park Headquarters.

Pedalai Trail

This is a short, easy trail covering only 1.8km (1 mile) and takes about 90 minutes to complete. It begins across the river from Naga Lubang Baya Longhouse near the Park Headquarters. You have to ascend 30m (98ft) up to the *Pendam Sepetang*, a traditional Iban burial ground dotted with old burial jars. The trail then follows the main ridge between Lubang Baya (crocodile pool) and Batang Ai River to its highest point, passing pig wallows and patches of forest cleared by the male Great Argus Pheasant for its mating dances. It then descends gradually to the top of Wong Padalai rapids, following the river downstream to a picnic area and the longboat pick-up point.

Bebiyong Trail

This 4km (2.5-mile) trail, which takes about 2½ hours to complete, starts at the Park Headquarters then on to the Bebiyong Mit stream, rising gradually to a height of 280m (919ft), leading to a resting point just below the ridge crest of Puncak Igau, offering excellent views of the surrounding forest. It then descends rapidly to the bank of Bebiyong Besai, a small river with crystal clear water cascading over gravel pools. The trail follows the river bank for about a kilometer to its confluence with the main Batang Ai River, the pick-up point for the boat back to Park Headquarters.

Belitong Trail

This moderately difficult trail of 4.6km (3 miles) follows the Padalai Trail for the first kilometer then continues upwards along the ridge crest to _Tuchong Belitong_, an important Iban burial ground site where the graves of six important tribal chiefs are located. The trail continues through fine hill forest, gaining height until it reaches Ulu Sungai Sekerong at 320m (1050ft). From here, an optional short but very steep climb leads to the peak of Tuchong Inggai at 420m (1378ft). This was an important lookout point during head-hunting days as the torches of enemy war parties moving up the Batang Ai River could easily be seen. A burial jar marks the final resting place of the famous warrior Tugang, whose spirit is said to guard the peak. The trail then descends steeply to the confluence of the Batang Ai River and the Lelayang stream, the pick-up point for the boat back to Park Headquarters. The trek usually takes about four hours. Wildlife is more likely to be heard than seen on the trek but various species of birds and squirrels can be spotted among the foliage. The boat journey back to the Park HQ passes through tranquil riverine scenery with kingfishers frequently diving into the river to catch fish.

Below: _The majestic Brahminy Kite, known as_ Singalang Burung, _is revered by the Ibans as their god of war._

Batang Ai NP & Lanjak Entimau Wildlife Sanctuary

Independent Travel

Independent travel to Batang Ai is fraught with uncertainty. It entails a 3½-hour bus trip to Sri Aman, a major town in the interior, followed by another 2-hour bus journey from Sri Aman to Lubok Antu , a small town 5km (3 miles) from the Hydro Lake. From here there is no public longboat transport to the lake, although you might be able to hitch a ride from local folk heading to Batang Ai. You might have to kick your heels for a day or two to meet someone going that way. However, if you do not have the time and don't wish to risk being stranded for days, it is advisable to arrange your trip through local travel companies in Kuching, the capital of Sarawak.

Enggam Trail

You have to be physically fit to tackle this 6-hour trek covering 8.2km (5 miles), which starts by following the Bebiyong trail to its highest point at Puncak Igau. It then continues up a steady climb for 1.9km (1.2 miles) through hill forest to reach Kota Enggam, a fortification built by the warrior Chieftain Enggam and his followers in their bid to resist the rule of the White Rajahs, the Brooke family from England, in the late 19th century.

Nowadays only traces of a defensive trench that protected Enggam's longhouse can be seen. The trail descends steadily for 600m (1969ft) to join the picturesque Bebiyong Besai River at Nanga Sengkulit longhouse. The trail then follows the river, occasionally through the stream itself, to rejoin the Bebiyong Trail at Nanga Sebabai Longhouse.

Sium Trail

The most strenuous but also the most rewarding of the five trails, this 5½-hour trek covering 7.6km (4.7 miles) starts from the bank opposite the Park Headquarters. The first 2.5km (1.5 miles) is a steady climb to the main Sium ridge at 415m (1362ft). The trail continues along this undulating ridge, passing through pristine hill forest until it reaches an Iban burial ground. Shortly afterwards it reaches the highest point, the peak of Bukit Sium Ukap at 704m (2310ft). The word *sium* in Iban means 'to sniff' as they refer to climbing very steep hills as 'sniffing the ground', indicating that the vertical terrain almost touches your nose when you climb the hill. A small area of ground has been cleared around a survey beacon at the peak and the unrestricted view is spectacular. The entire Batang Ai Hydro Lake and its surrounding forest are revealed in a green and blue panorama and on a clear day you can even see the distant Danau Sentarum lakes in Kalimantan, Indonesia.

The trail continues along the ridge for a short distance before descending rapidly to follow the Beritik River. A little further downstream is a majestic Tapang (*Koompassia excelsa*) tree; its massive white trunk with broad canopy high above the ground makes it an outstanding tree even in the rainforest. Wild bees favour its broad horizontal branches for their hives and the Ibans prize this tree as a source of honey. It would be taboo for them

Getting There and Accommodation

to fell the Tapang tree; doing so, they believe, would cause madness, delirium and death. From here, the trail continues along the Beritik River to its confluence with the Batang Ai where the boatmen take you back to Park Headquarters.

Getting there

Package tours to the park are offered by most tour operators in Kuching and these include overnight stays at longhouses, jungle safaris and camping in the forest. The Hilton Longhouse Resort at the lake offers the comfort of a five-star hotel with excursions near the lake and inside the park.

Batang Ai is located 275km (171 miles) east of Kuching and the journey over tar-sealed roads takes four to five hours. The road leads to the jetty at the edge of the hydroelectric dam reservoir and visitors will be ferried across the lake to reach the resort and park. The park is about an hour's boat ride upstream from the reservoir. During dry weather the water level is quite low and visitors may have to get out of the boat and help push it upstream – an experience that is more fun than work.

You can book your boat trips to the park at a floating coffee shop near the dam through representatives of the local co-operative. These passages are usually booked by the tour operators as part of the package. The journey to the park itself is a pleasant experience: when the boat enters the park it passes through a beautiful lowland forest of mixed dipterocarp, with drooping tree branches forming an overhanging green arch.

Accommodation

There is only a camping ground in the park and visitors usually stay at nearby Iban longhouses or at the Hilton Batang Ai Longhouse Resort.

What to bring

There is no canteen in the park so it is essential you bring enough food and water. Bring along swimming gear, good trekking shoes, comfortable cotton attire, suntan lotion, insect repellent and basic first-aid supplies. Campers have to bring their own camping gear. If you book a package tour, food is included in the price.

Useful Contacts

The Hilton Longhouse Resort (book through Kuching Hilton), tel: 6082 248 200, e-mail: batang-ai-longhouse@hilton.com For package tours, contact: Borneo Adventure, Kuching, tel: 6082 245 175, e-mail: info@borneoadventure.com website: www.borneoadventure.com Asian Overland Tours and Travel, Kuching, tel: 6082 451 309, e-mail: aoskch@po.jaring.my website: www.asianoverland.com.my For park enquiries and permits, contact: Sarawak Forestry, Level 11, Office Tower, Hock Lee Centre, Jalan Datuk Abang Abdul Rahim, 94300 Kuching, Sarawak, tel: 6082 348 001, fax: 6082 341 550, e-mail: info@sarawakforestry.com

National Park Booking Office, Visitor Information Centre, Jalan Tun Abang Haji Openg, 93000 Kuching, Sarawak, tel: 6082 248 088, fax: 6082 248 087.

Batang Ai National Park is open daily (including Sundays and Public Holidays) 08:00–12:30 and 14:00–17:15.

DANUM VALLEY CONSERVATION AREA, MALIAU BASIN AND TABIN WILDLIFE RESERVE

Sabah lies in the northeastern part of the island of Borneo with a coastline of 1440km (895 miles) of fine beaches on the west coast and mainly mangrove swamps on the east coast. Offshore there are 38 reef islands.

Known as 'Land Below the Wind' due to the fact that it lies just south of the typhoon-affected region, it is Malaysia's top adventure destination for ecological tourism. Its verdant forests harbour one of the world's most prolific biodiversities. Its national parks and conservation areas teem with wildlife, and a bewildering array of flora, many of which are rare species.

Top Ten

Hornbills
Borneo Bristlehead
Crimson Sunbird
Red-bearded Bee-eater
Scarlet-rumped Trogon
Orang-utans
Banteng
Sumatran rhinoceros
Pygmy elephants
Bornean gibbon

Opposite, top to bottom:
Fish frolicking at a water cascade, Tabin Wildlife Reserve; the Borneo pygmy elephant, the smallest elephant in the world; Borneo Rainforest Lodge, set along a picturesque river, offers comfortable accommodation in timber chalets for visitors to Danum Valley.

Danum Valley, Maliau Basin & Tabin Wildlife Reserve

Sabah

Danum Valley Conservation Area

Location: 66km (41 miles) from Lahad Datu.
Size: 438km² (169 sq miles).
Of interest: Jungle trekking, wildlife observation and canopy walk.

Sabah's forest can be divided into four types: coastal mangrove swamp, providing important habitats for fish and wetland birds such as egrets and herons and pivotal to the survival of the proboscis monkeys; lowland and highland dipterocarp forests, home to endangered species like orang-utans, elephants and rhinoceros; heath and limestone forest; and finally montane forest. Apart from mangrove swamp, the wetlands of Sabah include swamp forest, peat swamp forest, marshes, rivers and lakes, creating an ideal habitat for wetland birds and migratory flocks from as far as Australia and Siberia. It is also home to crocodiles and the false gharial. The marine habitat of Sabah is among the most diverse ecosystems on earth and its reefs are internationally known for pristine dive sites. The open sea is home to rich aquatic fauna including many valuable fish and invertebrates, as well as marine mammals such as porpoises and whales.

Although large tracts of rainforest have been cleared for commercial use, under the Wildlife Conservation Enactment of 1997 there are provisions for the declaration of three types of protected areas. The first of these is the Conservation Area, for the purpose of fast and flexible protection of wildlife and habitats. Another type, a Wildlife Sanctuary, is the strongest conservation category for fauna, flora, genetic resources and habitats. The third type is the Wildlife Hunting Area, intended for animal population management by regulated hunting. Currently a number of unique nature areas are in the process of being gazetted under these provisions in the Enactment. Among the many protected areas are the Danum Valley Conservation Area, Sabah's largest protected lowland forest; Tabin Wildlife Reserve, Maliau Basin Conservation Area and Kinabalu National Park.

Danum Valley Conservation Area

The Danum Valley forest reserve is a unique conservation area. It lies within the logging concession of the Sabah Foundation (Yayasan Sabah), an organization devoted to the welfare and education of the people of Sabah. In 1976, a scientific expedition led by the then Sabah National Park Board and funded by WWF Malaysia was carried out in the Danum area. The study discovered a real treasure trove of diverse wildlife and forest types and

Danum Valley Conservation Area

recommended that the area be gazetted as a national park. However, Sabah Foundation holds a 100-year logging concession in the area, but it conceded to designate the Danum Valley as a conservation area and in 1995 it was granted the status of Protection Forest Reserve, by which logging is prohibited by law. This illustrates that with the right vision and management, it is possible to strike a balance between conservation and commercialization of nature's bounty. It covers an area of 438km² (169 sq miles) and is managed by the Sabah Foundation, which set up the Danum Valley Field Centre (DVFC) in 1986 with a scientific faculty for the purposes of research, education, training and wilderness recreation. It has now become an internationally renowned tropical research faculty.

Above: The lowland rainforest with its cloak of lush vegetation is a magical sight when shrouded in the morning mist.

Danum Valley is surrounded by vast tracts of timber production forest but is protected by a wide buffer zone of natural forest on all sides, ensuring the wildlife's natural habitat can be sustained and preserved. Research in Danum Valley has discovered a bewildering variety of flora and an impressive menagerie of Sabah's lowland fauna, including such rare and endangered species as the Sumatran rhino, banteng or tembadau (Asian wild cattle), Asian elephant, clouded leopard, orang-utan and proboscis monkey. More than 120 mammals including 10 species of primates, 40 species of fish, over 300 species of birds, reptiles, amphibians and a profusion of butterflies are found here. Dipterocarp trees dominate the forest around Danum Valley Field Centre, with the canopy reaching a height of over 70m (230ft) in places. Some 90% of the Conservation Area is classified as lowland dipterocarp forest with the remaining 10% being low canopy, sub-montane forest mainly on Mount Danum in the heart of the Conservation Area.

Danum Valley, Maliau Basin & Tabin Wildlife Reserve

Call of the Wild

Set against such an enriched background, Danum Valley is one of the best conservation areas in Sabah for wildlife viewing, bird-watching, jungle trekking and nature study. Sadly the elusive and rare rhinoceros is hardly ever seen in the wild but happily the Asian elephant is frequently spotted here. The road leading to the Borneo Rainforest Lodge is littered with elephant dung and herds are often seen grazing by the roadside. 'Might is right' when encountering a herd of elephants, so keep a respectful distance and enjoy observing the pachyderm family interacting with one another, the matriarch keeping an eye on the youngsters while the patriarch of the herd stands guard in case you come too close. They are harmless if you keep a safe distance but as soon as the bull elephant flaps his ears and raises his trunk, it means you have outstayed your welcome and a hasty retreat is recommended.

Getting There

The nearest airport to Danum Valley is Lahad Datu, a short flight from Kota Kinabalu, the capital of Sabah. As Danum Valley is a restricted forest reserve area, trips into the park can only be booked through Borneo Nature Tours, the official agent for handling enquiries and reservations for the Borneo Rainforest Lodge. They will arrange transfers from the airport to the lodge, accommodation reservation, excursions and permits. The journey takes about two hours from Lahad Datu, with the first 15km (9 miles) on a sealed road along the main Lahad Datu to Tawau road and the remaining 66km (41 miles) on an unsealed (rough but well-maintained) private logging road. Danum Valley Conservation Area is located

Danum Valley Conservation

Lokan
Batu Puteh
Caves
Lamag
Pintasan
Kinabatangan
Labau
Tangkulap
Pinangah
Kaumut
BORNEO
RAINFOREST
LODGE
[H]
Danum Valley
Conservation Area
Pinangah
Kaumut
MALIAU
BASIN
Lotung
+
1666 m
Sabah
BANJARAN
BRASSEY
N
0   50 km
0   25 miles
Kalabakan
Serudong
Tawau Hills NP
Kalabakan
Tk.
Tawau
Merutai

Accommodation

across the Segama River, accessible by a timber bridge. Contact Borneo Nature Tours, Kota Kinabalu, tel: 6088 267 637; Lahad Datu, tel: 6089 880 207, e-mail: info@borneonaturetours.com website: www.borneorainforestlodge.net

Accommodation
Borneo Rainforest Lodge (BRL)

Set in a picturesque valley by the Danum River, the Borneo Rainforest Lodge offers a delightful base for jungle exploration in the Danum Valley Conservation Area. Located 40 minutes' drive from DVFC, the lodge was built to accommodate visitors in tranquil and remote surroundings. It is the only tourist facility in the area. The lodge was designed and constructed by naturalists out of local hardwood in the style of traditional local village dwellings. The resort has 24 low-rise, air-conditioned chalets housing 31 twin-sharing rooms dotted along the river, all with jungle or river views. A *belian* or hardwood walkway links the chalets to the main lodge which features a spacious open-plan layout with dining areas, bar and wide verandah overlooking the river and forested hill. This vantage point allows discreet observation of the riverside wildlife. Hornbills can be spotted flapping through the trees (they are not the most graceful of birds when in flight), while kingfishers and Oriental Darters frequently dive-bomb the river for fish. Squirrels and tree shrews dart up trees festooned with giant spiderwebs, the masterpieces of the golden orb weaver spider. Orang-utans, gibbons, slow loris, giant monitor lizards and even clouded leopards have been seen around the chalets. That is the beauty of the Borneo Rainforest Lodge – you can be an armchair naturalist just sitting on the verandah with a drink and nature comes to you.

To really appreciate the wondrous beauty of Danum Valley, you need to venture out on the trails. From the lodge, jungle trails can be arranged to the various places of interest. Nature guides will regale you with tales of the forest and point out the flora and fauna. Within an easy trek of the lodge is a 260m (853ft) long canopy walkway suspended 27m (89ft) above the ground, the best spot to watch birds close-up. Keep still and silent and some birds will land a wing flap away from you on the canopy of the trees. Among the avian denizens in Danum Valley are all of

Jangut The Bearded Mascot

You could be forgiven for thinking the local brew is making you hallucinate when you see a big bearded creature staring at you from the garden of the lodge. It is only the resident bearded wild pig nicknamed 'Jangut' ('beard' in Malay) foraging in the mud for food, occasionally glancing at guests with his beady eyes, expecting to be fed with morsels of food from their dining table. Jangut was born in the vicinity of the lodge and while his mother and siblings have returned to the wild, he opted for a more comfortable life. Although visitors are advised not to feed him, his porcine appeal is difficult to resist and he feasts regularly on leftovers, making him twice as big as his siblings living in the wild. Jangut is unlikely to make a speedy return to the wild as he revels in his privileged position as the resort's mascot and star attraction. He roams freely in the grounds of the lodge and looks tame but at heart he is still a wild animal and should not be approached or petted. He is certainly not a pet but a wily boar that has lost his fear of humans.

Danum Valley, Maliau Basin & Tabin Wildlife Reserve

Maliau Basin

Location: 190km (118 miles) from Tawau.
Size: 588.4km² (227 sq miles).
Altitude: 1675m (5496ft) escarpment area.
Of interest: Strenuous jungle trekking, night safari and a visit to the spectacular seven-tiered Maliau waterfalls.

Borneo's eight species of hornbills, Buffy Fish Owl, Borneo Bristlehead, Bulwer's Pheasant, plus all seven species of the colourful pitta, Crimson Sunbird, Red-bearded Bee-eater and Scarlet-rumped Trogon among many others. Attractions nearby include an ancient burial ground below the cliff overlooking the lodge and a natural 'jacuzzi' at the bottom of a waterfall, excellent for a dip after a hot trek. You can even float down the river over the slow rapids seated on a rubber inner tube.

The forest is beguiling by day and eerily enchanting at night. A night safari should not be missed. Visitors are transported by open-top vehicle fitted with a high seat for the guide who is equipped with a spotlight to search for the animals in the dark. Red eyes peering from the bushes reflect such nocturnal creatures as mousedeer and sambar deer, while in the treetops flying lemur and slow loris stare back, momentarily caught by the light while out foraging. The skill of the nature guides in spotting animals in the dark is amazing. Even a tiny bird asleep on a branch or a snake coiled up among the thick foliage does not escape the sharp eyes of the guides.

The night walk is another fascinating excursion. Bring a powerful torchlight and the guide will teach you the signs and ways of the wild by night. It is a magical experience to walk in the dark and be entertained by the sounds and sights of the forest.

Maliau Basin

Dubbed as the 'Lost World of Sabah', Maliau Basin Conservation Area was a hidden and mysterious wilderness until it was discovered nearly 30 years ago when a pilot flew over the area. Encircled by a formidable escarpment rising 1675m (5496ft) above sea level, the giant circular forested basin of 390km² (151 sq miles) is clad in pristine virgin forest harbouring a self-contained ecosystem never permanently inhabited by humans and with large areas still unexplored. Originally part of the Sabah Foundation timber concession, it was ceded to a Conservation Area for the purpose of research, education and training along with the Danum Valley Conservation Area about 60km (37 miles) to the east, when its unique natural history was discovered in 1988. The area was upgraded by the Sabah state government to a Class I Protection

Maliau Basin

Forest Reserve in 1997 and given legal status as a protected region forbidding logging activity. It was extended to its present size of 588.4km² (227 sq miles) by incorporating forested land to the east and north of the basin. In view of the many rare and new species of flora and fauna indigenous to the basin, it was further upgraded and gazetted as a cultural heritage site in 1999. To demarcate the boundary of legal logging areas, buffer zones surrounding the whole Maliau Basin Conservation Area were added to ensure the protection of the wildlife and their habitat.

The Conservation Area encompasses a diverse grouping of forest types, mainly lower montane forest, rare montane heath forest and lowland and hill dipterocarp forest. Dominated by majestic Agathis trees, the lower montane forest, which also contains oaks, laurels and conifers such as *Dacrydium* species, merges into mossy cloud forest on the northern rim. In the stunted montane heath forest, ant plants, rhododendrons and pitcher plants are common, while the lower montane forest are clad in *Dipteris* ferns along the river banks. Dipterocarp forest is found mostly on the Basin's outer flanks and in the interior valley bottoms, and is rich in fruit trees. Over 1800 species of plant have so far been identified, including six species of pitcher plants and at least 80 kinds of orchids. Several are new records for Sabah. The rare

Below: Trichoglottis smithii, a strikingly beautiful orchid endemic to Borneo and Sumatra, is commonly found in open or swampy forest.

Danum Valley, Maliau Basin & Tabin Wildlife Reserve

Borneo Pygmy Elephant

Borneo pygmy elephant *(Elephas maximus borneensis)* is a subspecies of the Asian elephant and is found only in Sabah and north Kalimantan. It is the smallest elephant in the world. Its origin is controversial: one hypothesis is that it is indigenous to Borneo, while the other proposes that it is descended from captive elephants imported in the 16th–18th centuries, which explains its passive nature. The Borneo elephants are dwindling in numbers due to loss of habitat and, in a survey in August 2007 by WWF, it was reported that there are no more than 1000 elephants left in Sabah. Steps are being taken to protect these magnificent beasts.

Rafflesia tengku-adlinii has also been found in Maliau Basin, one of only two known localities in Sabah, the other being near Trus Madi.

Animal Kingdom in the 'Lost World'

Undisturbed by man, the rich biodiversity in this hidden Eden harbours Sabah's most rare and endangered species, including Bornean pygmy elephants, orang-utan, proboscis monkey, clouded leopard, Malayan sun bear, banteng and bear cat. Other common species are wild boar, sambar deer, barking deer, mousedeer, leopard cat, gibbons, red leaf monkey and grey leaf monkey. A remarkable roll call of some 300 species of birds has been documented, including Bulwer's Pheasant, Giant Pitta, Bat Hawk, Bornean Bristlehead and eight species of hornbill, together with 24 species of birds newly recorded in the Maliau Basin, 5 Bornean endemic species and 2 migrant species. More than 35 species of amphibian have been found, including a frog species that makes its home in pitcher plants. Among the multitude of invertebrates found here, at least two species new to science – a water beetle *(Neptosternus thiambooni)* and a crab *(Thelphusula hulu)* – have been discovered.

Natural Wonders

An aerial view of Maliau Basin reveals a breathtaking vista of a sunken forest embraced by lofty cliffs that are punctuated with waterfalls. But the undisputed jewel in the crown of Maliau Basin is the awesome seven-tiered Maliau waterfalls cascading over and over into the Maliau River. The highest fall is 28m (92ft) high. Maliau is also the only place in Sabah with a non-oxbow lake in the form of Lake Linumunsut, located on the outer northern escarpment.

Visitor Information

Maliau Basin is suitable only for travellers who are physically fit and are enthused with a high spirit of adventure. It must be noted that Maliau Basin is a remote, rugged and isolated area with limited access, communication and safety facilities. There are 70km (44 miles) of marked trails within the Conservation Area and the treks are tough with many steep climbs and descents. A minimum of three days' trekking is needed to visit Maliau Falls

Accommodation

alone, and a minimum of five days to visit Maliau Falls, other smaller waterfalls and the montane heath forest. There are no roads inside the Conservation Area.

Getting There

Maliau Basin Conservation Area is located in south central Sabah, and is accessible via the towns of Tawau or Keningau, both four to five hours' drive away. Part of the journey is on rough, unsealed logging roads. The tour operator provides four-wheel-drive vehicles to ensure a safe and comfortable journey over rough terrain. At Maliau Basin Security Gate, where a Visitor Reception and Information building has been established, an access road leads to Agathis Camp and the Maliau Basin Studies Centre.

Accommodation

Accommodation is basic. At present it consists of a well-equipped campground at the Agathis Camp and at the two-storey Camel Trophy Camp. In addition, a range of satellite camps are linked by well-maintained trails within the Basin itself. Accommodation is restricted to these sites and visitors are not allowed to clear new camping areas.

Agathis Camp

Located some 20km (12 miles) to the north of the Security Gate at the southernmost edge of the Basin, this camp is set on the banks of a 15m (50ft) wide stream. A 1km (0.6-mile) self-guided nature trail at the camp provides visitors with an insight into the flora and fauna of the forest. The camp is well-equipped and offers basic creature comforts in hammock-style accommodation for up to 30 people, with electricity, toilets and showers.

Camel Trophy Camp

This two-storey building houses bunk beds, showers and solar electricity accommodating up to 15 visitors. Constructed by the Camel Trophy participants in 1993, it was the first permanent camp within the Basin and is located strategically at the crossroad of lower montane forest and the rare montane heath forest on Maliau's southern plateau. A 33m (108ft) high observation platform near the canopy of a large *Agathis borneensis* tree

Flight Duration to Gateway Points

Kuala Lumpur to Kota Kinabalu (capital of Sabah) – 2 hours 35 minutes.
Kota Kinabalu to Lahad Datu (the nearest airport to Danum Valley and Tabin Wildlife Reserve) – 55 minutes.
Kota Kinabalu to Tawau (the nearest airport to Maliau Basin) – 45 minutes.

Danum Valley, Maliau Basin & Tabin Wildlife Reserve

Sabah Foundation Conditions of Entry

• No hunting is allowed in Maliau Basin Conservation Area or Sabah Foundation Concession Area.
• Firearms are absolutely forbidden.
• No collecting or trapping of any plant or animal specimens unless with written approval from Maliau Basin Management Committee.
• No slashing of vegetation or cutting of new trails.
• No graffiti on rocks or trees.
• All litter must be brought out.
• All visitors must be accompanied by Sabah Foundation Forest Rangers, stay only in the designated campsites and take VHF radios with them.
• The only communication system which works here is VHF radios, allowing contact between Maliau Basin Conservation Area and the security gatehouse, Luasong Forestry Centre and Tawau. VHF sets can be hired from Sabah Foundation.
• Forest fires are a real danger and campfires can be lit only under the supervision of the Rangers.
• Maximum group size is 15 (10 is preferred) and each group must designate a leader and deputy leader.
• Visitors enter Maliau Basin Conservation Area at their own risk, and MUST show proof of Personal Accident Insurance Cover, including emergency helicopter evacuation, before permission is given to enter.

provides an ideal spot for observing birds at close range while enjoying a panoramic view of the towering canopies in the forest.

Belian Camp

This camp is about 25km (16 miles) from the Security Gate and within walking distance of the Maliau Basin Studies Centre. It has a camp site to accommodate 20 double tents, a large kitchen, shower room with toilets and a pavilion. Located in logged lowland dipterocarp forest near the banks of the Maliau River, it is close to an educational nature trail and a canopy walkway known as the 'Maliau Sky Bridge'.

Ginseng Camp

Sited near the 27m (89ft) high Ginseng Falls, this camp is about 5–6 hours' trek from Agathis Camp and can accommodate up to 20 people in hammock-style beds with toilet and shower facilities.

Seraya Camp

Located 4–6 hours' walk from Belian Camp, this is the night stop for visitors to the Maliau Falls. Trails around the camp pass a rare *Rafflesia tengku-adlinii* site.

Lobah Camp

Situated on top of a hill commanding a panoramic view of the Basin's rim, Lobah Camp is about 2km (1.25 miles) from Maliau Falls and serves as welcome pit stop for visitors from Ginseng and Camel Trophy Camps proceeding to the Falls.

Other satellite camps in remote locations, such as Rafflesia, Strike Ridge and Eucalyptus camps, are only accessible by helicopter. There are several helipads for use in emergency evacuation or for visitors who wish to fly into the Conservation Area rather than tackling the arduous treks.

Access to Maliau Basin Conservation Area is strictly controlled and permission to enter must be obtained in advance from the Sabah Foundation. It is advisable to arrange a tour to this area with a specialist travel company. Contact Borneo Nature Tours (see details under Danum Valley, page 107) who will arrange everything you need, including permits.

Tabin Wildlife Reserve

Tabin Wildlife Reserve

Nestled in the heart of the Dent Peninsula in eastern Sabah, Tabin Wildlife Reserve is one of the largest wildlife reserves in Malaysia. It covers a rectangular area of 1205km² (465 sq miles) of mostly secondary dipterocarp forest of former logged jungle with a central core of primary forest, flanked by oil palm plantations on the outer perimeters. It was gazetted as a wildlife reserve in 1984 primarily to protect the three largest endangered mammals in Sabah: the Sumatran rhinoceros, Borneo pygmy elephants and the banteng or tembadau, the Asian wild cattle. It is reputed to have the largest number of elephants in Sabah. The rhinoceros population is critically small and due to the vastness of the forest, they are too far apart to create a productive population, not to mention loss of habitat through commercial activities in the forest. Tabin Wildlife is the centre for research and education on the welfare of the rhinoceros through SOS Rhino, a non-profit international organization.

The habitat here is also home to a large number of mammals and birds, many of which are endemic and endangered. Its diverse fauna also includes sambar deer, barking deer, bearded pigs, sun bears, the illusive clouded leopard, mousedeer, civets and jungle cats (such as the beautiful leopard and marbled cats) and primates like the grey leaf monkeys, maroon monkeys and the ubiquitous and mischievous macaques. The feline fauna has an important role to play in nearby plantations by helping to keep pests like rats and other rodents in check in agricultural areas, highlighting the fact that it is important to retain pockets of forest areas near agriculture to maintain connectivity. It is in the interest of plantation owners to protect these jungle cats.

Fauna of the feathered kind are no less impressive, with a catalogue of birds that will please even the most ardent twitcher. A total of 220 species of birds from forty-two families have been recorded here. These include seven of the eight species of hornbill found in Borneo, plus other birds such as the Wren Babblers, Bornean Blue Flycatcher, Scarlet Sunbird, Everett's White-eye, the rare Speckled Piculet, Chestnut-capped Thrush, Thick-bellied Flowerpecker, as well as eagles and owls. Some of these species may be spotted around the resort in Tabin,

Tabin Wildlife Reserve

Location: 50km (31 miles) from Lahad Datu.

Size: 1205km² (465 sq miles).

Of interest: Jungle trekking, night safari and a visit to Lipad mud volcano for wildlife observation and personal 'beauty treatment'.

Danum Valley, Maliau Basin & Tabin Wildlife Reserve

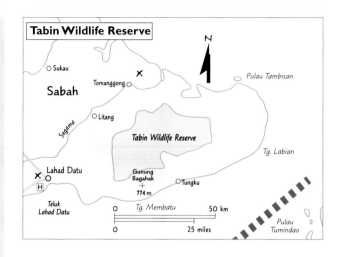

fluttering among the trees and flowers in the compound along with an array of butterflies.

Lipad Mud Volcano

All the usual jungle sports and activities are available in the reserve, but in addition Tabin also offers a unique trek to a mud volcano. There are three dormant mud volcanoes in the reserve, of which the second biggest – and nearest to the resort – is the Lipad mud volcano. It is accessible via a 2km (1.25-mile) trail over gentle terrain that gets very muddy when it rains. The resort provides rubber Wellington boots for visitors on the trail after a rainy spell.

On the way to the volcano, you may encounter plantain and pygmy squirrels or large tree-shrews scurrying among the branches, or you may be serenaded by birds with their birdsong echoing through the forest. The volcano spreads over a 2ha (5-acre) area and due to its high salt and mineral content is devoid of any vegetation. The active conical core of the volcano is a bubbling mass of grey mud oozing from a source deep in the ground. The mud is very rich in sodium and calcium and this is a favourite gathering point for mammals to wallow and lick the minerals to supplement their diet. Even birds have been seen pecking at the mud.

Lipad Mud Volcano

Elephants, sambar deer and bearded pigs are frequent visitors here. The animals leave calling cards on the mud plain in the form of footprints and droppings and the nature guides, who are forensic naturalists, will point out which animals they belong to. A five-storey observation tower has been constructed near the volcano to enable visitors to observe the animals without intruding into their space. The best time to wait in the hide is in the morning or late afternoon when the animals tend to gather in the cooler weather.

Night Safari Spotlighting

A favourite after-dinner activity in the resort is the night safari in a pick-up truck accompanied by a nature guide. The journey in pitch darkness traverses along palm oil plantation roads surrounding the reserve. The guide is equipped with a powerful spotlight to sweep the bushes and treetops looking for eyes reflecting out of the darkness. Momentarily blinded by the spotlight, the animals freeze in their tracks and visitors are able to catch a glimpse of these nocturnal creatures. Commonly spotted are civets and leopard cats, out on the prowl among the oil palm trees hunting for rodents, or owls perched on tree branches poised to swoop on their prey.

Above: Lipad Mud Volcano is a favourite haunt for the animals and birds that go there to supplement their mineral intake. It also attracts the human species as observers and for spa treatments.

Even if no animals are spotted, the safari in the dark forest is magical especially when the guide parks the truck and switches off the engine to allow visitors to enjoy the calls of the wild under a still starry sky, far from cities, civilization and neon lights. It is here that the ghostly, white bark of the majestic mengaris trees, which abound along the roads, casts eerie silhouettes against the star-lit forest.

Danum Valley, Maliau Basin & Tabin Wildlife Reserve

Banteng

The banteng, also known as *tembadau* in Sabah, is a member of the wild cattle family of Southeast Asia. This handsome ox is larger and more robust than domestic cattle and the male of the species can weigh up to a ton. The male banteng has a very dark brown or black coat, is armed with long, upwardly arched horns and has a hump over the shoulders. The female has a reddish brown coat, small horns pointing inward at the tip, and no hump. Both the male and female have distinctive white 'stocking' markings on their legs. Their natural habitat is usually hill forest where they feed on grass, fruits, bamboo and leaves. They move in herds like domestic cattle. The banteng is on the list of endangered species.

Saving The Rhino

SOS Rhino is a non-profit international organization dedicated to protecting rhinos and their habitat. To increase the understanding of the Sumatran rhinoceros, SOS Rhino has joined forces with Sabah Wildlife Department Malaysia, World Wildlife Fund (WWF), and Singapore Zoological Gardens (SZG) to form the SOS Rhino Team in Borneo. Over the years, it has built a successful SOS Rhino Borneo project in Tabin Wildlife Reserve for the purpose of 'research, education, marketing and advocacy'. Its Rhino Protection Units patrol the forest reserves of Borneo searching for the elusive pachyderm. In 2006, rangers out on patrol chanced upon a rhino and managed to film it on a handheld video camera, making it the first record of a rhino ever to be filmed in its natural habitat in Malaysia. Tracks of a baby rhino were also recently spotted in the heart of Borneo, allaying fears that this species is on the brink of extinction, though it is still highly endangered. According to SOS Rhino, the Bornean subspecies of the Sumatran rhinoceros is one of the most endangered rhinos – mainly due to habitat loss and poaching.

There may be as few as 30 of this subspecies left in the wild and only two in captivity in Sepilok for breeding and health evaluation. It is the smallest of the five species of rhino left in the world and is the only rhino species found in Malaysia. Research and data collection require large manpower resources and the Rhino Protection Units in Tabin engage villagers, plantation owners and their employees through the SOS Rhino's Community Outreach Programme. They welcome volunteers to help in their quest to secure the protection of this magnificent creature. SOS Rhino website: www.sosrhino.org

Getting There

Tabin Wildlife Reserve lies 50km (31 miles) northeast of Lahad Datu and there are daily flights from Kota Kinabalu. The transfer time to the reserve is about an hour and a half over an unsealed plantation road passing through large expanses of oil palm plantations and villages along the way. Visits to the reserve can be arranged through Tabin Wildlife Holidays Sdn Bhd. Contact them at tel: **6088 267 266**, email: enquiry@tabinwildlife.com.my website: www.tabinwildlife.com.my

Accommodation

Accommodation
Tabin Wildlife Reserve Lodge

Visitors to the reserve are accommodated in comfortable air-conditioned timber chalets built on a forested hill along the picturesque Lipad River. The buildings are constructed in authentic Borneo style to sympathetically blend in with nature. There are three categories of accommodation: 10 units of River Lodge bungalows in air-conditioned spacious twin/double-bedded rooms with *en-suite* bathroom/wc and balconies overlooking the Lipad River; 10 units of Hill Lodge bungalows in similar configuration as those at River Lodge, with balconies overlooking the Lipad River and the forest. Both lodges are connected via a timber walkway to the Sunbird Café which serves Asian and western food. Finally, there is an Eco Tented Platform (ETP), with comfortable tents erected on a platform above the forest floor and furnished with mattresses and mosquito nets, four people to each tent. There are four common shower rooms with toilets, two for females and two for males.

Above: A Sumatran rhinoceros wallowing in the mud is a rare sight due to its dwindling numbers, and great efforts are being made to protect these magnificent animals.

KINABATANGAN WILDLIFE SANCTUARY & SEPILOK ORANG-UTAN REHABILITATION CENTRE

Sabah is blessed with two of the most incredible wildlife attractions in Malaysia, where wildlife viewing is easily accessible to tourists, within easy reach of modern infrastructure yet contained within an authentic wild atmosphere. The Kinabatangan Wildlife Sanctuary and the Sepilok Orang-utan Rehabilitation Centre are arguably Sabah's most popular destinations to observe wildlife and they are usually arranged in the same tour package by local travel companies due to the proximity of the two destinations.

The Kinabatangan Wildlife Sanctuary along the Kinabatangan River has an astounding natural beauty. It is nature at its best, and rare species like proboscis monkeys, orang-utans and pygmy elephants are commonly spotted. It is an ecological Garden of Eden that should not be missed on a visit to Sabah. The Sepilok Orang-utan Rehabilitation Centre is another magical experience – to be up close and personal with orang-utans – and you have not lived till you've seen the 'men of the forest' in their natural surroundings.

Top Ten

Hornbills
Oriental Darter or Snakehead
Kingfishers
Storm's Stork
Grey-headed Fish Eagle
Orang-utans
Pygmy elephants
Proboscis monkeys
Estuarine crocodiles
Bearded pigs

Opposite, top to bottom:
An orang-utan constructs a new nest every night; an estuarine crocodile basks in the sun on the bank of the Kinabatangan River; dawn safari on the oxbow lake off Kinabatangan, a great excursion for bird-watching and wildlife observation.

Kinabatangan & Sepilok Rehabilitation Centre

Kinabatangan Wildlife Sanctuary

Kinabatangan Wildlife Sanctuary

Location: 135km (84 miles) from Sandakan.
Size: 270km² (104 sq miles).
Of interest: Dawn and late afternoon river safaris for game viewing and bird-watching.

For centuries the Kinabatangan River has been the lifeblood of the local people, mostly Orang Sungai. It was the conduit for communication, water supply, irrigation and trade of such forest products as edible birds' nest, bees' wax, elephant ivory and hornbill casques. The forest was plundered by bounty hunters before the advent of conservation law. In the 1950s the area was allocated for large-scale logging and by the 1970s mono-cash crop agriculture was practised as thousands of hectares of dipterocarp forest were cleared for commercial oil palm plantations which now dominate the landscape. Loss of habitat and human intrusion into wildlife territory has led to conflict between animals and plantation staff and it could end in the extinction of many endangered species. A dialogue has been exchanged between non-governmental organizations (NGOs) like WWF, plantations, small landholders and government authorities to maintain forested areas alongside the river, thus creating riverside wildlife corridors to connect fragmented forest. The future survival of the wildlife population in the Kinabatangan effectively lies in the hands of the plantation owners and others.

The Kinabatangan flood plain is the last bastion for the survival of one the richest and most fragile biodiversities on earth, and the Kinabatangan Wildlife Sanctuary was gazetted to protect these resources. A fragmented area of 26,103ha (64,501 acres) with 12,000ha (29,652 acres) of forest reserve forms a narrow forested corridor, now protected under the wildlife sanctuary. The Kinabatangan is the largest and longest river in Sabah, lazing its way in ox-bow loops across 560km (348 miles) of channels through a catchment area of 16,800km² (6485 sq miles) of flood plain. It covers almost 23% of the total land area of Sabah, originating in northwest Sabah in the Crocker Range and flowing eastwards to the Sulu Sea on the east coast. Flooding is common along the river, with a mean rainfall of 2500mm (99in) to 3000mm (118in) per annum.

The Kinabatangan flood plain is the largest remaining forested flood plain in Sabah and the lower stretches of the Kinabatangan River contain some of the few surviving freshwater swamp rainforests and oxbow lakes in Southeast Asia. These evergreen

Sandakan

Kota Kinabalu to Sandakan (the nearest airport to Sepilok and Kinabatangan River) – 40 minutes. Sandakan was the capital of former British North Borneo (the old name for Sabah). In 1945, the Japanese destroyed the town and the capital moved to Jesselton (now Kota Kinabalu). Today it is a bustling fishing port and is famous for its seafood and the Agnes Keith Museum, where the author used to live. It is preserved as it was when she left Sabah after the war.

Kinabatangan Wildlife Sanctuary

swamp rainforests are of global significance and known internationally for their biodiversity – mixed saltwater mangrove forest, riverine forest and dipterocarp forest, where the diversity of plant and animal life is intense. A large part of the region remains unexplored and much of the plant and animal life along the river has yet to be fully studied.

A Natural Treasure

The diverse and fragile ecological system of the Kinabatangan flood plain is home to rare and endangered animals. A thousand plant species, 250 bird species, 90 fish species, reptiles and 50 mammal species have been recorded in the lower Kinabatangan. It is one of only two known places on earth where 10 primate species can be found. These include the orang-utan, and several species of primates endemic to Borneo, such as the proboscis monkey, the maroon langur and Bornean gibbon. Other primates include silvered leaf monkeys or langurs and macaques. Sharks and rays, usually thought of as sea creatures, have been discovered by scientists in the upper reaches of lower Kinabatangan but little is known about them. Other animals found here are the Borneo pygmy elephants, civets, a variety of snakes, estuarine crocodiles, otters and wild boars. The rich bird life includes the Oriental Darter or snakehead, herons, egrets, Wallace's Hawk-Eagle, Jerdon's Baza, Violet Cuckoo, Blue-eared Kingfisher, Grey-headed Fish Eagle, eight species of hornbills, Bornean Bristlehead and the threatened Storm's Stork. The much hunted estuarine crocodile – the largest crocodile species in the world – has become extremely rare, but can sometimes still be seen basking along the river banks or lurking in the river.

Above: The silvered leaf monkey is a shy primate, unlike the raucous macaques. Its baby is born bright orange and turns dark grey as it gets older.

River Safari

The Kinabatangan Wildlife Sanctuary is perfect for tourists who like to enjoy wildlife-based adventure without having to rough it on arduous treks in the jungle. The forest around the village of

Kinabatangan & Sepilok Rehabilitation Centre

Sukau is an ecological Eden where at dawn and in the late afternoon the creatures of the forest come out to parade on the lush river banks, especially along the Menanggul River, a small tributary of the Kinabatangan where the wildlife is abundant.

Nature watching begins in the late afternoon on a wide-bottomed river safari boat accompanied by a nature guide and boatman. The graceful Oriental Darter swoops into the river and comes up with a shimmering fish in its beak. The ubiquitous White Egret, abundant in the area, stands statue-like on a floating branch ready to stab at an unsuspecting fish. On the drooping branches, playful macaques indulge in noisy horseplay. In the thick foliage, green Wagler's pit vipers and yellow-ringed cat snakes can occasionally be seen coiled in camouflage, visible only to the trained eye. (The snakes pose no threat to visitors unless provoked; despite their bad press, snakes are in fact seldom dangerous.) Hornbills, usually in pairs, are often spotted perched on a branch, preening. A rare sight is the Asian Paradise Flycatcher with its splendid blue tail plumage catching the sun in the dappled light.

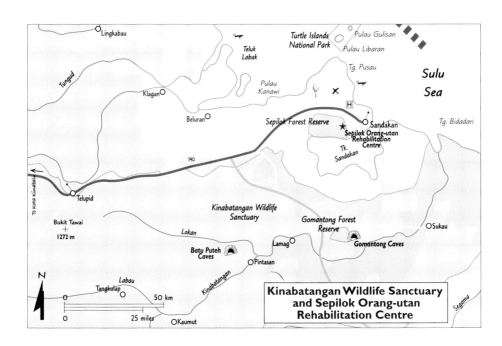

Dawn River Safari

The joker of the jungle is the raucous, squawking proboscis monkey that colonizes the mangrove forest along the Kinabatangan. These primates, endemic to Borneo, move in large noisy groups usually led by an alpha male presiding over his harem of females, babies and youngsters. They feed on the young leaves of *Sonneratia* trees growing in abundance along the river bank and never fail to make an appearance on every river cruise. The male proboscis is a charismatic beast endowed with a pendulous nose and rotund belly; it makes loud guttural calls. The female is much smaller and possesses neither the pendulous nose nor the big belly. Their two-tone fur is red on the back and head and cream on the chest, belly, tail and the small of the back. Their red hair and big noses have earned them the name of *Kera Belanda* or 'Dutchman monkey', a local nickname likening them to early sunburnt, fair-haired missionaries. The proboscis monkeys have no fear of humans.

Herds of the Borneo pygmy elephant, sometimes numbering 30 or 40, graze or swim along the river. The elephants tend to ignore the presence of humans as long as they keep their distance.

Dawn River Safari

This is another magical experience. The boat journey starts early, when the forest is swathed in mist as it rises off the river and infiltrates the forest canopy. Flashes of colour catch the sun as kingfishers dive for their breakfast while hornbills, with their noisy wingbeats, emerge from their roosts high in the canopy. A flock of rare Storm's Storks flies high above the canopy like a squadron of fighter jets. Resting on a branch, the majestic Fish Eagle surveys the forest for prey. This is the best hour for bird-watchers.

The morning safari takes visitors to an ox-bow lake about 30 minutes away. The boat negotiates small streams through bowers of trees. Snakes with beautiful markings and colours are sometimes seen among the branches. The ox-bow lake is a tranquil body of water surrounded by lush forest alive with the sound of birds. With luck you may see orang-utans hiding among the thick foliage. In the wild, they are shy but not nervous animals, unlike monkeys, which tend to be quite jumpy and noisy. It is a privilege to see these sedate and very endangered apes in the wild.

Bounty of the Cave

The Gomantong Caves lie about 10km (6 miles) from Sukau and are easily accessible by road from the village. The caves are home to millions of bats and swiftlets whose nests are much prized by the Chinese for bird's-nest soup. The cup-shaped nests are made from the saliva of the birds and are cemented to the roof of the caves. Collectors construct a system of bamboo ladders to reach the roof of the caves from where the nests are removed. The nests can fetch up to several thousand ringgits per kilogram. The Chinese believe the birds' nests are nutritious and health-enhancing, though there is no scientific proof to support this theory. The guano of the bats and swiftlets supports a huge colony of invertebrates, and the cave floor heaves with millions of cockroaches, earwigs and crickets.

Kinabatangan & Sepilok Rehabilitation Centre

Getting There

A leisurely two-hour boat journey from the town of Sandakan through mangrove and nipah forests takes visitors to the village of Sukau on the lower Kinabatangan River where timber lodges dotted along the riverbank provide simple and comfortable accommodation. This is the base camp of the wildlife sanctuary. There is no public transport and local travel companies will arrange the whole trip including boat transfers, accommodation, full board and river safari. It is possible to travel to Sukau by road through a very rough and dusty oil palm plantation road from Sandakan and it takes two uncomfortable hours. As a result, tour operators opt for the river journey. Operators and river lodge owners are encouraged to practise responsible tourism in the Kinabatangan Wildlife Sanctuary and to strike a balance between mass tourism and conservation of the fragile environment in the area.

Below: A female orang-utan nurtures its baby until at least five years old, when it may leave its mother to live an independent and solitary life.

Accommodation

There are eco-friendly lodges in Sukau offering rooms with ceiling fans, mosquito netting, *en-suite* bathrooms with hot showers, and restaurants that serve good Asian food.

Sukau Rainforest Lodge (operated by Borneo Eco Tours) Contact: Borneo Eco Tours, Kota Kinabalu, tel: 6088 438 300, e-mail: info@borneoecotours.com website: www.borneoecotours.com This 20-room eco lodge has all the comforts, including solar-heated showers, set in the rainforest and fronted by the river. Facilities include three bird and wildlife viewing decks and 457m (1500ft) of a covered 'Hornbill Broadway' into the forest, complete with corridors in the vegetation to accommodate elephants on their regular treks through the forest at the back of the lodge. A video presentation and short talk are given by a nature guide after dinner.

Sepilok Orang-utan Rehabilitation Centre

Kinabatangan Riverside Lodge (KRL) (operated by S.I. Tours)
Contact: S.I. Tours, Sandakan, tel: 6089 673 502 or 673 503,
e-mail: sitours2@tm.net.my website: www.sitoursborneo.com
A 22-room chalet complex with *en-suite* bathroom/wc/hot
shower stocked with 'biodegradable and environmentally friendly
shampoo, soap and paper', mosquito netting, ceiling fan and
restaurant. A video presentation and a short talk are given by a
nature guide after dinner. S.I. Tours is one of the main operators
to the Kinabatangan Wildlife Sanctuary and they own a fleet of
fibreglass river boats to ply guests between Sandakan and Sukau.
They also own the Abai Jungle Restaurant and Lodge at Abai
Village, an hour away from Sandakan, halfway to Sukau. This
18-room lodge has *en-suite* bathrooms/hot showers, mosquito
netting and ceiling fans. Guests may opt to stay the night here to
break their journey.

Proboscis Lodge Sukau (operated by Sipadan Dive Centre)
Contact: Sipadan Dive Centre, Kota Kinabalu, tel: 6088 240 584,
e-mail: sdc@sipadandivers.com website: www.sipadandivers.com
Chalet-style accommodation set amid the forest near the
Menanggul River, all rooms with *en-suite* bathroom/hot shower,
ceiling fan and mosquito netting. The restaurant serves local food.
River safaris can be arranged at the lodge.

Sepilok Orang-utan Rehabilitation Centre
The Sepilok Orang-utan Rehabilitation Centre is one of the
best-known orang-utan rehabilitation centres in Southeast Asia
due to its easy accessibility. Set at the edge of the Kabili-Sepilok
Forest Reserve in an area of 43km^2 (17 sq miles) of lowland
dipterocarp forest, it was first established in 1964 under the
Forestry Department, until 1988 when the administration and
management was given over to the new Wildlife Department of
Sabah. The primary aim of the centre is to rehabilitate displaced
orang-utans. Since its inception, the centre has encouraged a
greater local and international awareness of endangered species,
resulting in an increase in detection and confiscation of illegally
held captive animals. The objectives of the project have expanded
in recent years to include public education on conservation,
research and assistance to other endangered species such as
captive breeding of the rare and endangered rhinoceros. It also

Borneo Eco Tours

Borneo Eco Tours operates tours
within Sabah and Sarawak. For every
guest who travels to Sukau with
them, Borneo Eco Tours contributes
U$1 to the community, and
environmental projects under the
Sukau Ecotour Research &
Development Centre (SERDC)
include wildlife rehabilitation, a tree
planting project, medical project
and other activities to benefit the
local people.

**Sepilok Orang-utan
Rehabilitation Centre**

Location: 25km (15 miles)
from Sandakan.
Size: 43km^2 (17 sq miles).
Of interest: Close encounters with
orang-utans during feeding times
twice a day at Platform A at Sepilok.

Kinabatangan & Sepilok Rehabilitation Centre

Sepilok Mangrove Forest Trail

The 5km (3-mile) Mangrove Forest Trail runs from the Rehabilitation Centre over sandstone ridges into the mangrove forest on the boundary of the reserve. The trail passes scenic streams, water holes, transitional forest, pristine lowland rainforest, and a boardwalk into the mangrove forest leads to Sepilok Laut. The one-way journey takes about 2–3 hours and you can arrange to return by boat. The forest is under the control of the Forestry Department and a permit has to be obtained before proceeding on the trail. Boats as well as accommodation in the forest can be arranged through the department. Visitors should enquire at the Visitor Reception Centre at Sepilok for more information about the trail.

provides a veterinary service to other wildlife such as sun bear, gibbons and sometimes even elephants. The full complement of the rehabilitation centre is now under the supervision of more than 37 staff, including a Wildlife Officer who is officer-in-charge of the centre, a veterinary doctor and wildlife rangers. It has an animal clinic, a quarantine area and enclosures for animals such as the rhinoceros.

Rehabilitation

The rehabilitation process comes in three stages and it begins immediately after an orang-utan has been admitted to the centre. All animals are given a thorough general health examination shortly after arrival, followed by a quarantine period of 3–6 months to eliminate the possibility of them passing diseases to other orang-utans. Throughout the rehabilitation process, the animals are closely monitored for any health problems. The medical check-up comprises tests for TB and malaria, urine analysis, bacteriology and a chest X-ray. After quarantine, the orang-utan will be assessed as to whether it should undergo the whole programme or start from the second or third stage, depending on progress made.

Nursery School

Human nursery schools teach children to interact and play with other children. Young orang-utans, aged between one and three years, undergo a similar period of 'pre-school' training to give them skills essential to survival in the wild, such as the ability to climb trees and explore the use of their limbs. In the wild, young orang-utans spend the first five years of their lives with their mothers, learning the skills of survival. Captive orang-utans, deprived of their mothers, are unable to find food, build nests, or even climb properly. Contrary to the belief that primates are born to climb, baby orang-utans have to be taught. The centre sets up a nursery to encourage the animals to develop climbing skills under the watchful eye of rangers who have assumed the role of 'surrogate mothers', but are always mindful not to grow too attached to their wards. Like children, orang-utans need companionship, and the centre has a buddy system where the young apes are paired with older ones to encourage and teach them the art of living in the wild. They often develop very close relationships and help each other in their learning process.

Sepilok Orang-utan Rehabilitation Centre

Platform A (Outward Bound School)

After graduation from the nursery and as they grow older, orang-utans go through a period at 'Outward Bound School' where their dependence on the food and emotional support given by the rehabilitation centre is gradually reduced. Here, orang-utans are given increasing freedom and at the same time encouraged to learn to fend for themselves. At platform A, their natural forest diet is supplemented with milk, added minerals and vitamins, and fruits twice a day. This deliberately monotonous diet is fed to them every day in the hope that they will get bored with the food and will start to forage for themselves in the wild.

This platform is open to visitors, and you can watch the orang-utans from a raised timber deck a few feet away but at a safe distance. The platform is accessed via a timber walkway about 10 minutes' walk from the centre's reception. No food or drinks are allowed on the walkway or platform as this will distract the orang-utans. Occasionally the orang-utans will be overcome by curiosity and will wander among the visitors, but handling and petting of the animals is not permitted. Apart from the possibility of passing disease to them and vice versa, they may look cuddly but they are wild at heart and prone to unpredictable behaviour. Watch out for nimble fingers, as they are quick to grab cameras, hats and bags if they see an opportunity to do so. If an orang-utan snatches anything from you, do not attempt to take it back yourself – call one of the rangers to retrieve it, since they are trained to handle the apes. Daily feeding times are 10:00 and 15:00, but 10:00 only on Fridays.

Platform B (Going Back to the Wild)

The rehabilitation process is complete when an orang-utan has totally adjusted itself in the forest and shows signs of independence. It is gradually transferred to the last phase of survival training at Platform B, located further away from the centre. To encourage independence, the apes are slowly weaned off the food being fed to them, in order to force them to look for food in the forest. Here most animals eventually achieve total independence and become integrated into Sepilok's wild orang-utan population. Since the Centre was established, more than 100 orang-utans have been successfully released.

Getting to Sepilok Orang-utan Rehabilitation Centre

The Sepilok Orang-utan Rehabilitation Centre is situated on the east coast of Sabah, 23km (14 miles) from Sandakan at Batu 14, Jalan Labuk. Sandakan can be reached from Kota Kinabalu by a 45-minute daily flight with Malaysian Airlines. If you are not booked on a tour, take a taxi to the centre. Public buses do not go right up to the centre but stop at the junction 1.5km (1 mile) away.
Opening hours are as follows: Security Gate, daily from 08:00–17:00; Reception and Ticketing Counter, daily from 09:00–11:00 and 14:00–15:30; Exhibition Hall, daily (except Fridays) from 09:00–16:30; Centre, daily from 09:00–12:00 and 14:00–16:00, Fridays 09:00–11:00 and 14:00–16:00.
Admission Rates: adults RM30, children under 18 RM15. The use of cameras, camcorders and phone cameras will be charged at RM10.00

KINABALU NATIONAL PARK

South China
Sea

Tuaran

Kota Kinabalu

Kinabalu
National Park

Sabah

Kudat

Keningau

Kinabalu National Park is one of the most picturesque national parks in Malaysia, blessed with rugged mountain ranges and valleys cloaked in lush rainforest often shrouded in cloud and mist. Established in 1964, it is the first UNESCO World Heritage Site to have been designated in Malaysia, in December 2000, for its 'outstanding universal values as a centre of plant diversity in Southeast Asia and for its diverse biota and high endemism', making it one of the most important biological sites in the world. The park is dominated by the majestic Mount Kinabalu, the highest mountain in Southeast Asia, rising to 4101m (13,455ft), a mountain cloaked in mystery and legend.

Top Ten

Mountain Black Eye
Whitehead's Trogon
Kinabalu Friendly Warbler
Kinabalu Serpent Eagle
Bornean Mountain Whistler
Malay sun bear
Western tarsier
Bornean gibbons
Prevost's squirrel
Kinabalu ferret-badger

Opposite, top to bottom: The peak of Mount Kinabalu, with its Donkey's Ears, is an iconic rock formation in Sabah; upper montane forest is characterized by gnarled trees, stunted shrubs and rhododendrons; the fearsome Low's Gully, which the Kadazans nicknamed 'the Place of Death'.

Kinabalu National Park

Kinabalu National Park

Location: 90km (56 miles) from Kota Kinabalu.

Size: 754km² (291 sq miles).

Altitude: 1500m (4922ft) at Park Headquarters, 4101m (13,455ft) at peak of Mount Kinabalu.

Of interest: Jungle trekking and summit climb to the peak of Mount Kinabalu.

Park Regulations

Please follow the regulations while you are in the park. Under the Sabah Parks Enactment of 1984 it is an offence to:

* kill, capture, disturb or remove any animal, nests or eggs.
* remove, damage or set fire to any vegetation or any object of geological, historical or other scientific interest.
* bring any plant or animal into the park.
* deface or write on any rocks, trees or buildings.

These regulations protect the park for your benefit, the benefit of your children and for future generations.

Kinabalu National Park

The park has four different types of altitudinal forests, all exceptionally rich in tree and plant species. The lowland is clad in mixed dipterocarp forest rising to lower montane forest with oaks, laurels, myrtles and conifers at an elevation of 1200m (3937ft) to 2350m (7710ft). At 3000m (9843ft), upper montane forest dominates, characterized by glorious rhododendrons on the slopes of Mount Kinabalu. As the altitude increases, alpine meadow becomes apparent, with moss-covered gnarled, stunted trees and shrubs, until it reaches the treeline at between 3350m (10,991ft) and 3700m (12,140ft), after which no vegetation grows on the steep rocks of the summit. More than half of all Borneo's flowering plants and the majority of its mammals, birds, amphibians and invertebrates can be found in Kinabalu National Park.

Flora and Fauna

Kinabalu National Park is a naturalist's paradise, whether you are a budding ornithologist, entomologist, botanist, zoologist or just a nature lover. There are 5000 to 6000 plant species comprising 200 families and 1000 genera. The mountain is famous for its wide variety of carnivorous plants – nine *Nepenthes* species including the *Nepenthes rajah*, the largest known pitcher plant with a 2-litre capacity, and the jug-shaped Low's pitcher plant (*Nepenthes lowii*). There are an estimated 1500 species of orchids of which 77 are endemic to the park, including five species of slipper orchids of the genus *Papiopedillium*. There are 608 fern species, 24 rhododendron species (5 endemics), 52 palm species, 30 ginger species, 10 bamboo species, 78 ficus species (over 50% of the 135 species found in Borneo) and three species of Rafflesia.

The mammal inhabitants are categorized into 92 lowland species and 22 montane species, notably tarsiers, Malay sun bear, orang-utans, Bornean gibbons, grey leaf monkeys, red leaf monkeys, bay cat and the Kinabalu ferret-badger among others. Amphibians include 61 frogs and toads; 100 species of reptiles, 40 species of fish belonging to 9 families; 290 species of butterflies and 112 species of 'macro' moths. It is also a bird-watcher's paradise with 326 species representing more than 50% of all bird species found in Borneo. They belong to three groups: lowland, montane and subalpine. Most commonly spotted are Mountain Black Eye,

Park Attractions

Mountain Black Bird, Bornean Treepie, Kinabalu Friendly Warbler and Kinabalu Serpent Eagle, in addition to the Crimson-breasted Wood Partridge and Bornean Mountain Whistler.

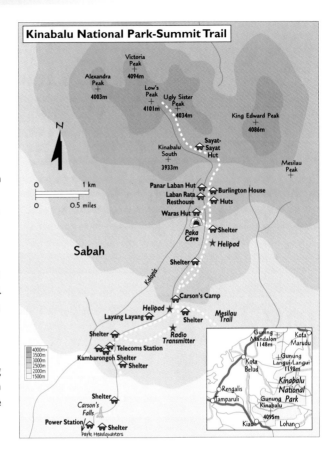

Kinabalu National Park-Summit Trail

Park Attractions

Kinabalu National Park is 90km (56 miles) from Kota Kinabalu, a two-hour scenic drive over a good sealed road. The road leads right up to the Park Headquarters situated 1500m (4922ft) above sea level on the southern boundary of the park. The 754km^2 (291 sq mile) park offers several graded walking trails including seven ridge-top and two stream-side trails leading to caves, scenic viewing points, waterfalls and mountain streams. The cool temperature at this altitude is perfect for exploring the jungle. If you are planning to embark on the summit trail and have no time constraints, first explore the jungle surrounding the Park Headquarters. There are guided trail walks along gravel paths and timber walkways around the park. The park naturalists will explain the park's flora and fauna. The mountain garden, enclosed in a 2ha (5-acre) area in natural surroundings, is a good introduction to the flora of the park. Watch out for exotic species such as Kinabalu nutmeg, kerosene trees, earth fig, climbing bamboo, Kinabalu balsam, lipstick flower as well as wild and rare orchids and ginger plants. There is an orchidarium showcasing the various orchids found in the park, including one of the smallest orchids in the world, the squat moss orchid (*Bulbophyllum minutissimum*) whose minute flowers measure only 4–5mm (0.16–0.2in). The mountain garden will give you a preview of the type of natural habitat you will find on the summit trail with its beautiful foliage, flowers and small streams. Squirrels and tree shrews scurry up the trees, birdsong fills the air and the beauty of the colourful butterflies distracts and delights. In the evening there is usually a video presentation and talk by park naturalists to educate visitors on the natural history of Kinabalu.

Kinabalu National Park

The moods of Mount Kinabalu change at the whim of the weather, one minute shy behind the cloud and mist, another moment splendidly showing off its strange rocky formations. Then, without warning, the mood becomes threatening and unforgiving. It has tasted blood: people have died on this mountain, though thankfully few. It is a mountain shrouded in mystery and legend and anyone who enters its domain does so on the mountain's own terms. Legend has it that a Kadazan maiden fell in love with a visiting Chinese prince and bore him a son. Her lover had to return to China, but promised he would come back for her and their son. Every day she would stand at the highest point in Sabah to look out for the ship that would bring her prince back. But alas, he perished in a shipwreck and never returned. Heartbroken, mother and son were turned into stone. Hence, Mount Kinabalu is also known as 'Kina Balu' or the 'Chinese Widow.' The Kadazans call it 'Aki Nabalu', 'the revered resting place of the dead', and treat it with deep respect. Here sacrificial offerings are made to the spirits each year.

There are comfortable forest cabins and lodges with all amenities, including fireplaces around the Park Headquarters.

Mount Kinabalu

Hailed as one of the highest peaks in Southeast Asia, Mount Kinabalu is an internationally renowned iconic landmark of Sabah, and indeed the whole of Malaysia. Geologically speaking, it is the youngest non-volcanic mountain in the world, a mere baby of only one million years. From a distance, it stands sentinel over Sabah, its awesome granite massif dominating the landscape. Its majestic beauty is alluring and it seduces both young and old to pay homage. It attracts people from all walks of life, from the competitive athlete and endurance sports enthusiast to those who are simply mesmerized by this enigmatic mountain. To the Kadazan-Dusuns, the largest indigenous tribe in Sabah, who dwell in villages at the foot of the mountain, the mountain belongs in the realm of the gods and is the final resting place of their loved ones. Thousands of experienced as well as novice climbers have scaled the mountain, ranging in age from the youngest, reputedly three years of age, to the oldest at 80 years. Mountaineering skill is not essential but physical fitness, good health and a strong stamina would be advisable as the climb is challenging.

The Summit Trail

The highlight of a visit to the park is the summit trail to 'conquer' Mount Kinabalu. There are two trails leading to the summit. The most popular and shorter trail is via the Timpohon Gate – it takes four to six hours to reach the first base at Laban Rata resthouse – and the second is longer albeit more scenic, the Mesilau Trail. Cool mountain air refreshes climbers throughout the trail, and there are several shelters for resting along the way.

To get to the start of the summit trail, you can travel by vehicle or walk from the Park Headquarters on the Kamborongoh Road for 4km (2.5 miles) to the Power Station at 1829m (6000ft). The Timpohon Gate signals the start of the summit trail, marked at intervals of 5 chains (50 chains = 1km), running past the Power Station, which follows a narrow ridge onto the main slope of Mount Kinabalu, covered mostly in montane oak forest. A short distance away is Carson's Falls, named after the first warden of

Mount Kinabalu

Left: Temperate clime plants like wild raspberries are found at high altitude (around 6000ft) on Mount Kinabalu.

What You Need to Bring for the Climb

the park. Here the moss-clad vegetation is punctuated with rhododendron shrubs and, when in bloom, they set the forest aglow with their vivid colours. *Dawsonia*, one of the largest moss species in the world, is commonly found here, and can grow to a height of 1m (3ft).

After Carson's Falls, the ascent rises steeply, accessed via step-like tree roots, to the first summit trail shelter at 1951m (6401ft). The path continues to climb sharply up a narrow ridge before dipping into a mossy forest with gnarled and twisted branches festooned with mosses, ferns and orchids, reaching the second shelter at 2134m (7000ft). Low's pitcher plants are found here, named after Hugh Low, a British colonial officer, who in 1851 was the first man to record his ascent of the mountain, though he failed to reach the summit.

The trail continues, offering shelters at various elevations, through bamboo forest including Miss Gibb's Bamboo (*Bambusa gibbsiae*), a tall delicate climbing plant that wraps itself around a tree for support. It was named after British botanist Lillian Gibbs who visited Sabah in 1910 and was the first woman to climb the mountain. Several species of tree ferns abound here, and birds like the Yellow-breasted Warbler and Mountain Bush Warbler are commonly spotted among the bamboos and ferns; occasionally the Kinabalu Friendly Warbler also makes an appearance.

suitable walking shoes
warm clothing
windbreaker
long-sleeved shirts
change of clothes
drinking water
high-energy food (chocolates, nuts, raisins, glucose)
headache tablets
sun block
lip balm
deep heat lotion
plasters
insect repellent
mosquito oil
binoculars
camera in waterproof bag
torchlight
extra socks
towel
gloves
hat
tissue paper
toilet roll

Kinabalu National Park

Local Travel Companies

Borneo Adventure, Kota Kinabalu,
tel: 6088 238 731 or 238 732,
e-mail: infokk@borneoadventure.com
Borneo Eco Tours, Kota Kinabalu,
tel: 6088 438 300,
e-mail: info@borneoecotours.com
**Asian Overland Services Tours
and Travel**, Kota Kinabalu,
tel: 6088 212 170,
e-mail: aosbki@po.jaring.my

Below: Aptly named, the Donkey's Ears is one of the most iconic rock formations on Mount Kinabalu, standing out like ears listening to the wind.

At 3353m (11,000ft) Panar Laban base camp is reached and most people stay overnight at the Laban Rata hostel, which has electricity, hot water, heated rooms and a restaurant. There is other more basic accommodation without room heaters in Panar Laban. Here the pioneer explorers first stopped to make a sacrificial offering of a white cockerel and seven eggs to appease the mountain spirits in accordance with local belief. Today, the ritual is carried out once a year.

The final assault of the summit starts in the early hours of the morning to catch the sunrise at the peak. From Laban Rata the trail climbs up a gully to the last and highest shelter, at 3810m (12,500ft), at Sayat-Sayat, named after the 'sayat-sayat' bushes (*Leptospermum*), which grow in profusion in the area. White mountain necklace orchids (*Coelogyne papillosa*) dangle out of rock crevices like snowy garlands around the camp. The vast expanse of the granite massif, which forms the summit, looms ahead, revealing the stark beauty of the place as the trail leads upwards between South Peak and St John's Peak on the left and the Donkey's Ears and the Ugly Sisters on the right. Low's Peak, the summit itself, is not visible at this point until the upper part of the summit plateau is reached. Most ascents are planned in time to see the first golden rays of the day on top of the world, confirming why the Kadazans believe that this mountain belongs to the realm of the gods.

On a clear day, much of Sabah is visible before clouds shroud the mountain again, usually at 09:00 or 10:00 when it is time to begin the descent. From here, you can see the fearsome Low's Gully, a 1.25km (0.8-mile) deep chasm which became headline news in March 1994 when five British soldiers attempted to explore the gully, nicknamed by the Kadazans as 'the Place of Death', and got lost for nearly four weeks before being rescued by Malaysian soldiers.

Climbing Mount Kinabalu

Preparation for the Summit Climb

Climbers should respect the mountain and be prepared for its unpredictable weather. Dress appropriately in wind- and waterproof clothing and pack spare clothes and shoes in plastic bags to keep them dry. Trainers are adequate for climbing. All climbers to the summit must be accompanied by registered guides. Familiarize yourself with the naturalist programmes at the Park Headquarters before you set out on the expedition. Book a guide and porter (if required) through the park's Head Office in Kota Kinabalu. Reservations cannot be made at the Park Headquarters itself. If you do not have your own transfer vehicle, remember to arrange for transport to take you to and from Timpohon Gate at Power Station Road where the climb starts.

Sabah Parks, Kota Kinabalu
tel: 6088 211881 or 212 719
e-mail: info@sabahparks.org.my
e-mail: sabahparks@sabah.gov.my

SPECIAL NOTE:

It is recommended that all climbers should have themselves medically checked before attempting any mountain climb. If you have a history of suffering from the following ailments, or any other disease which may hamper the climber, it is highly recommended that you refrain from climbing: hypertension, diabetes, palpitations, arthritis, heart disease, severe anaemia, peptic ulcers, epileptic fits, obesity (overweight), chronic asthma, muscular cramps, hepatitis (jaundice).

Accommodation

For accommodation at Kinabalu National Park (private chalets and lodges), Mesilau (lodges) and Laban Rata (resthouse and huts), most with heated showers, contact:

Sutera Sanctuary Lodges
G15, Ground Floor, Wisma Sabah, 88000, Kota Kinabalu, Sabah, Malaysia, tel: 6088 243 629 or 6088 245 742
e-mail: info@suterasanctuarylodges.com
website: www.suterasanctuarylodges.com
(online booking is available)

Visitor Information

• Kinabalu National Park is located in Kundasang, 90km (56 miles) from Kota Kinabalu, a 2-hour journey. Buses and taxis ply the route from Kota Kinabalu. Opening hours: 07:00–22:00.

• **Bus:** Look for buses with Kundasang-Ranau service at the Long Distance Bus Station near Merdeka Field (Padang). Fare (one-way): RM18 per person. To catch the return bus from the park, wait across the road outside the Park Headquarters (reconfirm with reception counter). Buses operate from 07:30–17:00.

• **Taxi:** Service from Ranau taxi stand next to Merdeka Field. Approximately RM160 per taxi (shared with other passengers) or RM300 per taxi if pick-up from hotel lobby for sole use. For return journey, book taxis at the reception counter at Park Headquarters. Buses and shared taxis will only leave when they are full.

• **Car Rental:** Approximately RM180 per day per car. Check with hotel concierge for local car rental companies. International driving licence required.

• The most convenient and fastest way to visit the park and climb Mount Kinabalu is to book through local travel companies (*see panel, page 134*).

SIPADAN ISLAND AND PULAU TIGA NATIONAL PARK

O ff the southeast coast of the Dent Peninsula in Sabah lie a cluster of islands collectively known as the Semporna Islands. Among the cluster is one of the top five best dive sites in the world, Sipadan Island. When Jacques Cousteau, the late oceanographic scientist and pioneer scuba explorer, visited the island in 1989 aboard his research ship, *Calypso*, he was captivated by its pristine beauty and diverse marine life and famously declared, 'I have seen other places like Sipadan, 45 years ago, but now no more. Now we have found an untouched piece of art'. That single remark placed Sipadan in the limelight of other 'celebrity dive sites'. It is a diver's paradise.

Top Ten

Turtles
Barracuda
Sharks
Manta ray
Bumphead parrotfish
Megapodes
Green Imperial Pigeons
Pied Hornbills
Magpie Robins
Sunbirds

Opposite, top to bottom:
Sipadan Island offers one of the best dive sites in the world; a sea krait (Laticauda colubrina) *enjoying a big mouthful of eel at Pulau Kalumpunian Damit near Pulau Tiga; clown fish live with sea anemones for mutual benefits, each protecting the other from predators.*

Sipadan Island and Pulau Tiga National Park

Sipadan Island

Sipadan Island

Location: 35km (22 miles) south of Semporna, which in turn is 350km (218 miles) from Kota Kinabalu.

Size: 16.4ha (40 acres).

Of interest: Acclaimed as one of the best dive sites in the world by Jacques Cousteau.

Diving at Sipadan

There are local tour operators who specialize in diving tours to Sipadan and other dive sites in Sabah as well as conducting diving courses (beginners to advanced PADI). They will arrange transportation from Kota Kinabalu or Sandakan, accommodation on the nearby islands and diving schedules.

Borneo Divers, Kota Kinabalu, tel: 6088 222 226, e-mail: Reservations@BorneoDivers.info website: www.BorneoDivers.info (operates Mabul Island Resort).

Pulau Sipadan Resorts, Tawau, tel: 6089 763 575, e-mail: kapalai@tm.net.my Sandakan branch, tel: 6089 673 999, e-mail: sepilok@po.jaring.my (operates Kapalai Island Resort).

Sipadan Dive Centre, Kota Kinabalu, tel: 6088 240 584, e-mail: sdc@sipadandivers.com website: www.sipadandivers.com

Sipadan was first gazetted as a bird sanctuary in 1933 and its wild remoteness attracted few visitors until sport divers rediscovered it in the late 70s. At first only a few divers knew and had access to this Eden but as its reputation grew, Sipadan became the top spot on every serious diver's wish list. Its geographic location puts the island within the Indo-Pacific basin, the richest marine biodiversity area in the world. Marine scientists are still discovering new species as new places and depths are explored.

Sipadan is the only oceanic island in Malaysia formed from an extinct volcanic cone. It rises from a depth of over 600m (1969ft) from the ocean floor, mushrooming to the surface as a tiny island surrounded by a reef and powder white beach with a small enclave of virgin forest in the centre. The drop-off zone at the edge of the reef is dramatic, its vertical fall fortified by overhanging rocks. The walls are encrusted with coral while the ledges along the sheer drop provide resting places for turtles. Beyond the reef rim at the reef crest, sharks, turtles and the whole spectrum of tropical marine life abound. Wall divers will be entranced by the technicolor world of soft coral gardens showcasing big sea fans, black corals, *Dendrophyllia* coral, sponge barrels and a plethora of other colourful species. Small butterfly fish, damselfish and groupers as well as bigger species like snappers, surgeonfish, whitetip reef sharks, turtles and manta rays are found here. In the nooks and crannies live coral fish like whitetip and jewfish, and also other micro creatures. Down the submerged wall, the mysterious Turtle Cavern is infiltrated by a labyrinth of channels and tunnels and strewn with the skeletal remains of turtles, perhaps trapped and entombed when they strayed into the cave.

Cave diving is a special skill and non-cave divers should not attempt to explore this cave. The current can be strong here and it is advisable to stay close to the wall and follow instructions from the dive masters.

Diving spots in the area have been given names to identify their locations. The most popular diving spot at Sipadan is Barracuda Point. The visibility is generally good here from 20–30m (66–98ft) but currents can be unpredictable and the site is not recommended

Sipadan Island

for novice and inexperienced divers. Large fish species, like leopard shark and whitetip sharks, and turtles are commonly encountered here, but it is renowned for its large shoal of chevron barracuda, which sometimes circle near divers, blocking out the sunlight with its density.

Divers usually ascend via Coral Gardens, an amazing underwater garden, landscaped with soft and hard corals of every shape and colour, which harbours a variety of coral inhabitants such as whitetip sharks,

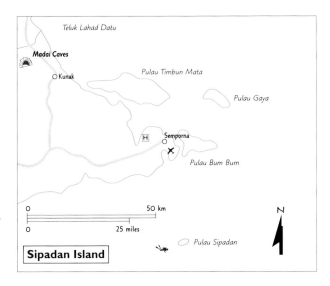

schools of trigger fish, angel fish, various species of wrasse (including the giant Napoleon), surgeonfish and unicornfish. Mantis prawns, spider crabs and the showy blue ribbon eel can be spotted among the corals. The currents tend to be a bit tricky and only experienced divers should attempt this dive.

At South Point, with an average depth of about 20m (66ft), the strong current tends to attract pelagic species coming in to feed on the plankton, together with patrolling reef sharks and skirting manta rays. It is quite common to encounter big shoals of fusiliers, batfish, snappers, rainbow runners and sweetlips among other colourful coral denizens. Large schools of trevally and hordes of marauding bumphead parrotfish liven up the scene. Other less skittish species like lionfish, crocodilefish, pufferfish, green turtles and hawskbill turtles join in the parade. Occasionally, the awesome whale shark has been spotted by some lucky divers.

Sadly, the pristine aspect of Sipadan is also its liability. The sheer number of recreational divers invading the island throughout the years has taken a toll on the marine life and the beauty of the island. Uninformed divers have been known to rest on corals, flapping their flippers carelessly on delicate corals and dislodging them. Marine biologists have raised concern over the impact of mass tourism on such a small island. The Sabah state government has stepped in to conserve the island as a fully protected zone by ordering all the resorts on Sipadan to be closed and the numbers of divers restricted. Sabah Parks have stationed their personnel on the island to keep guard and guests are restricted to areas close to the jetty only. Visitors to Sipadan are now ferried there by dive operators at scheduled dive times, while accommodation has been moved to the nearby islands of Mabul (25 minutes away), Kapalai (18 minutes away) and Mataking (80 minutes away).

Sipadan Island and Pulau Tiga National Park

Pulau Tiga National Park

Location: 50km (30 miles) from Kota Kinabalu.
Size: 158km² (61 sq miles).
Of interest: Scuba diving, jungle trekking and a visit to neighbouring Pulau Kalampunian Damit (Snake Island) to observe sea kraits in their nesting ground.

Marine Life

Pulau Tiga's unspoilt marine habitat supports a wide variety of marine life. Without the onslaught of mass tourism, it is a tranquil place to dive and snorkel. *Dendronepthya* soft coral, gorgonian sea fans, sea pens, barrel sponge, elephant ear sponge and tube sponge thrive here. Molluscs such as tiger cowrie, the poisonous textile cones, nudibranchs, thorny oysters, giant clams, cuttlefish and reef octopus lurk among the corals. Mantis shrimps, transparent shrimps, painted rock lobsters and hermit crabs hide in the crevices among the corals. There are 132 species of fish in the waters here including marbled stingrays, giant moray eels, clownfish, lionfish, chevron barracuda, spotted sweetlips, Moorish idol, batfish, tattooed parrot fish and a variety of kaleidoscopic species.

The best time to dive in Sipadan is during the dry season between April and November, with July and August the best diving months. During the rainy season and with the strong current, visibility is not great but divers who are into 'muck diving' will not be disappointed. Sipadan is generally more suitable for experienced divers due to its vertical topography and unpredictable currents. When diving in Sipadan, respect the sea and its treasures and stay close to your diving masters who are skilled in reading the current. If every diver consciously makes an attempt to conserve Sipadan's unique wild beauty, this marine paradise will be around in perpetuity. Work is currently in progress to list Sipadan as a UNESCO World Heritage Site.

Pulau Tiga National Park

Pulau Tiga or 'Three Islands' belongs to a group of three small islands 10km (6 miles) off the west coast of Sabah in the Kimanis Bay opposite the Klias Peninsula. Its claim to fame is as location for the television series *Survivor*. Of the three islands, Pulau Kalampunian Besar has been reduced to a mere sandbar while Pulau Kalampunian Damit, also known as Snake Island, is just a rocky outcrop, its undisturbed habitat the breeding ground for thousands of amphibious sea kraits. These are venomous snakes but do not usually pose a threat to divers unless provoked.

Pulau Tiga's name is a misnomer in that it is not called after the three islands but refers to the three volcanic mud hills dominating the island. It is the largest of the three islands and covers an area of 158km² (61 sq miles) of pristine virgin rainforest fringed by white sandy beach and the warm turquoise waters of the South China Sea. Due to its marine biodiversity and varied terrestrial ecosystem, it was protected as a forest reserve in 1933 and was gazetted as a marine park in 1978. Mass tourism has not quite reached the island yet; this hidden off-the-beaten-track jewel offers great diving and snorkelling sites, while its unspoilt forest, which harbours a rich variety of flora and fauna, can be explored through a network of jungle trails. One of the trails, a 30-minute trek, leads to a cold bubbling mud volcano produced by gas rising from the earth, causing loud burping sounds at frequent intervals, splattering mud around the vegetation. It is popular with visitors who plaster themselves with the mud as a beauty treatment.

Pulau Tiga National Park

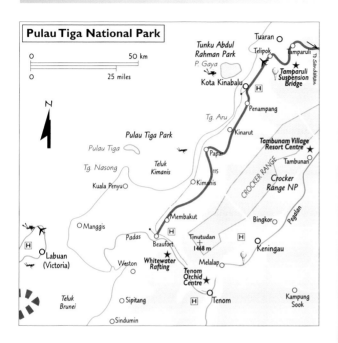

Getting There

Pulau Tiga is 50km (31 miles) south of Kota Kinabalu and can be reached by boat from there or via Kuala Penyu, 140km (87 miles) away by road followed by a 45-minute boat ride. The best time to visit is February to April when it's dry and the sea is calm.

Accommodation

Accommodation on the island is provided by Pulau Tiga Resort which offers comfortable air-conditioned rooms with *en-suite* bathrooms, a restaurant and barbecue facilities. Activities at the resort include scuba diving, snorkelling, jet-skiing, kayaking, banana boat riding and fishing. For reservations and travel arrangements, contact: Sipadan Dive Centre, Kota Kinabalu, tel: 6088 240 584, e-mail: pultiga@tm.net.my or sdc@sipadandivers.com

Permits for the island can be obtained from Sabah Parks Office in Kota Kinabalu. If you are travelling with a tour company, they will normally apply for your permit as part of your package.

Flora and Fauna

The island's flora is luxuriant mixed forest. On the shoreline, casuarina trees colonize the sand, along with native trees like *Barringtonia*, which are festooned with flamboyant pink and white night-flowering blossoms when in bloom. The roots of these trees are often used by ground-dwelling megapodes to hatch their eggs. This chicken-like greyish brown bird with a bare red face has enormous feet to build nesting mounds in which to incubate its eggs. Morning glory grows in profusion around the casuarinas. In the interior, *ranggu* and *keruing* trees dominate the forest, along with local fruits such as rambutans, mangosteens, jambu, figs and langsat. Strangler figs grow in abundance and the fruits are favourites of the Pied Imperial and Green Imperial Pigeons. In the southern fringe of the forest is a mangrove lagoon. The forest fauna includes bearded pigs, long-tailed macaques, monitor lizards and skinks, while airborne forest dwellers such as Pied Hornbills, nightjars, megapodes, Magpie Robins and sunbirds as well as bats and flying foxes are commonly found.

NATIONAL PARKS GUIDE

Other Malaysian National Parks

Tanjong Datu National Park

Location: Southwestern tip of Sarawak on Datu Peninsula in Kuching division.

Size: 1379ha (3408 acres). Gazetted in 1994.

Attractions: Remote location, pristine forest fringed by a beach with crystal clear water and patches of coral, ideal for snorkelling, scuba diving and dolphin spotting. Rich in wildlife such as Bornean gibbons, pig-tailed and long-tailed macaques, silvered and banded langurs, bearded pigs, sambar deer, mousedeer, bear cats and civets; numerous species of bird in mixed dipterocarp forest, including Peacock Pheasants and three types of hornbills. Nesting ground for green turtles and Olive Ridley marine turtles.

Similajau National Park

Location: 30km (19 miles) northeast of Bintulu in Sarawak.

Size: 8996ha (22,229 acres). Gazetted in 1979, extended in 2000.

Attractions: A pristine park, blessed with a stretch of golden beach. The forest teems with wildlife. There are 185 species of birds and 24 species of mammals including gibbons, long-tailed macaques, leaf monkeys, wild pigs, mousedeer, civets, porcupine, squirrels and shrews. Reptiles include the endangered estuarine crocodiles, false gharial and various species of snakes. Dolphins, horseshoe crabs, hawksbill, green turtles and occasionally the rare leatherback turtle make up the marine attraction.

Lambir Hills National Park

Location: 32km (20 miles) from Miri in northeast Sarawak.

Size: 6952ha (17,178 acres). Gazetted in 1975.

Attractions: Interesting topography of sandstone hills with rugged terrain, some rising to 450m (1476ft), and scenic waterfalls and pools. Its complex ecosystem makes it an excellent centre for rainforest environmental studies by scientists who are stationed in the park. It is rich in bird life with 237 species at last count and various species of monkeys, deer, gibbons, wild boars and flying squirrels to name a few. Challenging trails through picturesque landscape with water features and diverse vegetation.

Heart of Borneo Declaration

On 12 January 2007, leaders of the three Bornean governments, namely Brunei Darussalam, Indonesia and Malaysia, officially endorsed an agreement to conserve 220,000km² (84,920 sq miles) of equatorial rainforests known as the 'Heart of Borneo'. It recognizes its importance as one of the most significant centres of biological diversity in the world, supporting the habitat of 13 primate species, more than 350 bird species, 150 reptiles and amphibians, and around 15,000 species of plants. The Heart of Borneo is one of only two places on earth where rhinos, elephants and orang-utans co-exist, and new discoveries are still being made, with an average of three new species discovered every month over the past 10 years alone.

Opposite, top to bottom:
The scenic waterfalls are one of the main attractions at Lambir Hills National Park; green turtles (Chelonia mydas), common in the waters of Malaysia, can live up to 80 years old; a white sandy beach on the idyllic island of Perhentian.

National Parks Guide

Loagan Bunut National Park

Location: 120km (75 miles) from Miri in northeast Sarawak.
Size: 10,736ha (26,529 acres). Gazetted in 1991.
Attractions: The park centres round Sarawak's largest natural lake, which covers an area of 65ha (161 acres). The cyclical nature of the lake provides a unique aquatic ecosystem, influenced by the cycle of flood and drought. The lake supports both aquatic and terrestrial creatures. When the water is low in February, late May and early June and July, most aquatic species will swim into the Bunut River which connect the Tinjar and Baram rivers while fish and shrimps trapped in the shallow pools provide a feast for the birds and bountiful catch for the Berawan indigenous tribe who lives in the area. This is the best time for bird-watching, and resident species such as eagles, swallows, malkohas, Stork-billed Kingfishers, magpies, robins, doves, Racquet-tailed Drongos, Pied Hornbills and kites are joined by visitors including the Oriental Darter, egrets, herons, bitterns and storks.

Penang National Park

Location: Nestled against the border of the capital city of Georgetown and the sea on the north-west corner of the island of Penang.
Size: 2563ha (6333 acres) including beach, hill and sea. Gazetted in 1980.
Attractions: Flora, fauna and marine life which includes 1000 species of plants, 148 species of birds of which the most commonly spotted are White-bellied Sea Eagles and kingfishers, 28 species of

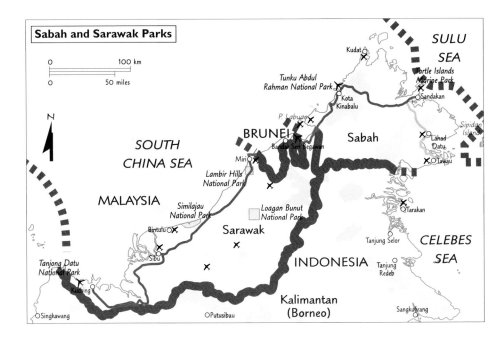

Other Malaysian National Parks

mammals, and 14 species of reptiles. Long-tailed macaques are dominant along the beach and mangrove forest. Trekking on challenging trails and swimming on the beach are popular activities. A 126-step path leads to an observation tower with a panoramic view of Teluk Bahang and Batu Ferringhi.

Tanjung Piai National Park

Location: Located 75km (47 miles) from the city of Johor Bahru, it is the most southernmost tip of mainland Asia in the southern state of Johor.
Size: 926ha (2288 acres) of which 526ha (1230 acres) are coastal mangrove forest.
Attractions: The mangrove forest is a diverse and intriguing ecosystem of complex vegetation. A network of wooden walkways into the mangrove swamps allows visitors to observe the wildlife at close range, to see mangrove crabs, mudskippers, crab-eating macaques and monitor lizards. Avian residents include Spoon-billed Sandpipers, Lesser Adjutant Stork and myriad seasonal migratory birds, notably whimbrel, Common Redshank, Greenshank and Grey Plover among others.

Tunku Abdul Rahman National Park

Location: This cluster of five islands is a 20-minute boat ride from Kota Kinabalu in Sabah.
Size: 4929ha (12,180 acres) of which two-thirds are covered by sea. Gazetted in 1974.
Attractions: The five islands are all named symbolically after their historical connections: Pulau Gaya (Big – the biggest of the five islands); Pulau Manukan (Fish – for its rich marine life), the most developed of the islands with comfortable chalets and restaurant, managed by Sutera Harbour Resort in Kota Kinabalu; Manutik (Shells – for its abundance of sea shells); Sapi (Buffaloes) and Sulug (after the Sulu people of Sabah). All the islands are fringed with sandy beaches and the crystal clear waters teem with marine life and exotic corals. Main activities are snorkelling, diving and picnicking. The fauna includes long-tailed macaques, pangolins, wild boars and a variety of birds – most commonly spotted are Sea Eagles, sandpipers, flycatchers, sunbirds, Pied Hornbills and Great Crested Terns.

Turtle Islands Marine Park

Location: Comprises three islands 40km (25 miles) north of Sandakan in Sabah.
Size: 1740ha (4300 acres) including surrounding sea and coral reefs. Gazetted in 1977.
Attractions: Pulau Seligan, second largest of the three islands and location of the first turtle hatchery in Sabah set up in 1966 to protect turtles that nest on the island. It is the most developed of the three islands, with accommodation for visitors who can watch green turtles coming ashore to lay eggs. Numbers are restricted to 38 people per night. Pulau Gulisan, the smallest of the three islands, is home to hawksbill turtles. Pulau Bakkungan Kecil, largest of the three islands, has a bubbling mud volcano in the centre and is home to green turtles.

Pulau Payar Marine Park

Location: Located in the northern part of the Straits of Malacca, 30km (19 miles) from Langkawi island in the state of Kedah, a 45-minute ferry ride away.
Size: 2km (1.25 miles) long and 0.25km (0.16 mile) wide.

National Parks Guide

Attractions: It is equipped with a huge floating platform moored off Pulau Payar with a restaurant and facilities for showering and changing. There is no accommodation on the island and only daytrippers are allowed. The platform is the base for swimming, snorkelling and scuba diving. It also has an underwater chamber for visitors to view the marine life without getting wet. The best diving is along the south, east and west of the island. There is a sandy beach and shallow waters where baby sharks and other fish gather around swimmers. On the southern tip of the island, a coral garden by the reef is inundated with multicoloured corals.

Pulau Tioman Marine Park

Location: 44km (27 miles) northeast from Mersing in Johor, but the island lies in the state of Pahang. There are fast ferry services between Mersing and Pulau Tioman.
Size: 39km (24 miles) long and 12km (7 miles) wide.
Attractions: It is surrounded by beautiful sandy beaches and sheltered coves and has one of the best dive sites in the area. The rocky outcrops of Pulau Labas, Pulau Tokong Bahara and Pulau Gut, part of the sister islands, have the best reef and marine life, with multicoloured soft corals. The rainforest harbours 45 mammal species including sun bears, long-tailed macaques, slow loris, giant black squirrels, red giant squirrels, mousedeer, brush-tailed porcupines and common palm civets; 138 bird species including the frigatebird; and rare soft-shelled land turtles and the peculiar mud skippers that live on the shoreline and wriggle about in the shallow water.

Pulau Redang Marine Park

Location: 50km (31 miles) off the coast of Kuala Terengganu, a journey by boat, speedboat or double-decker catamaran from the coastal town of Chendering.
Size: 25km² (9.5 square miles)
Attractions: The Redang archipelago consists of nine islands: Pulau Redang, Pulau Pinang, Pulau Ling, Pulau Kerengga Besar, Pulau Kerengga Kecil, Pulau Paku Kecil, Pulau Paku Besar, Pulau Lima and Pulau Ekor Tebu, each blessed with powder-white sand and turquoise waters heaving with marine life and spectacular soft corals of many hues, boasting 55 genera of corals and 100 species of fish.

Pulau Perhentian

Location: 20km (12 miles) off Kuala Besut in Terengganu, off northeast coast of Malaysia. The islands are served by public boat service from Kuala Bersut 2km (1.25 miles) from Kuala Terengganu.
Size: Comprises two islands – Pulau Perhentian Besar at 950ha (2348 acres) and Pulau Perhentian Kecil at 630ha (1557 acres) – set among a cluster of rocky islets.
Attractions: The name 'Perhentian' means 'stopover', referring to its historical role as a resting point for ancient traders and fishermen and, in more recent times, even a stopover point for migratory birds. Perhentian is part of the Redang National Marine Park and both islands are framed by white sandy beaches with forest-clad interiors. The crystalline waters are ideal for swimming, snorkelling and scuba diving. The sea is a haven for reef fish, sharks and colourful corals, black corals and nudibranchs. Turtles come ashore to lay eggs between April and September.

Other Malaysian National Parks

Krau Wildlife Reserve

Location: Halfway between Jerantut and Temerloh in western Pahang.

Size: 60349ha (149,122 acres) of primary forest reserve set up in 1968 as a research site for field studies of the flora and fauna of the reserve.

Attractions: Second largest wildlife protected area after Taman Negara, covered in lowland, riverine and montane forests providing habitats for feline species like tiger, clouded leopard, leopard, marbled cat, leopard cat, fishing cat, flat-headed cat, Asiatic golden cat and civets, also mongoose, otters, monkeys and gibbons. Bird life is luxuriant and 190 species have been recorded, notably the Giant Pitta, Malaysian Peacock Pheasant, White-bellied Woodpecker, owls, frogmouths, Crested Wood Partridge and Crested Fireback Pheasant. In the canopy are eight species of hornbills, bulbuls, barbets, pigeons, broadbills, leafbirds, sunbirds and all the species of lowland forest.

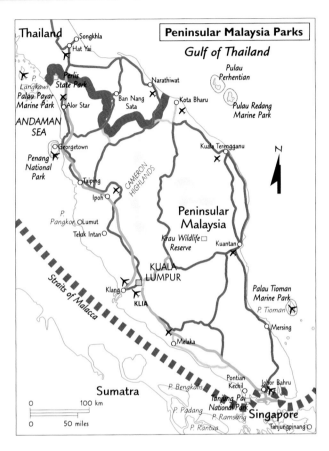

Perlis State Park

Location: In the state of Perlis, 30km (19 miles) from Kangar, the state capital.

Size: 5000ha (12,355 acres) of semi-deciduous forest.

Attractions: A continuous limestone hill range called the Nakawan Range is 36km (22 miles) long. The hilly landscape has pointed limestone peaks sweeping down steep cliff faces into hidden valleys and caves, traversed by streams. The park consists of Mata Ayer and Wang Mu Forest Reserves and includes the caves of Gua Burma and Gua Kelam, with 380m (1246ft) of lighted suspended boardwalk running through the cave. The rare stump-tailed macaque with its unique red face and red bottom is an endemic primate species found only in this park in Malaysia. There are over 30 species of mammals and 200 species of birds, including six kinds of hornbills, and at least 49 reptiles and amphibians.

Travel Tips

Tour companies who operate nature tours in Malaysia:

Asian Overland Services Tours and Travel, 39C & 40C Jalan Mamamda 9, Ampang Point, 68000 Ampang, Kuala Lumpur, Malaysia, tel: 603 4252 9100, e-mail: aos@asianoverland. com.my website: www.asianoverland.com.my

Ping Anchorage, 27A, Jalan Wawasan, Ampang 2/1, Bandar Baru Ampang, 68000 Ampang, Selangor, tel: 603 4280 8030, e-mail: klso@ping anchorage.com.my website: www.pinganchorage.com.my

Journey Malaysia.com, Dolphin Diaries Sdn Bhd, No. 9 Lorong San Ah Wing, Off Lorong Gurney, Jalan Semarak, 54100 Kuala Lumpur, tel: 603 2692 8049, e-mail: pappy@journey malaysia.com website: www.journeymalaysia.com

Borneo Nature Tours, Block D, Lot 10, Ground Floor, Sadong Jaya Complex, 88100 Kota Kinabalu, Sabah, tel: 6088 267 637, e-mail: info@borneonaturetours.com website: www.borneonature tours.com

Borneo Adventure, 55 Main Bazaar, 93000 Kuching, Sarawak, tel: 6082 245 175, e-mail: info@borneoadventure. com website: www.borneo adventure.com

Intra Travel Service, Level 1, Office No. 5, Airport Terminal 2, Old Airport Road, Kota Kinabalu, Sabah, tel: 6088 261 558, e-mail: enquiry@ intra-travel.com.my website: www.intra-travel.com.my

Useful Addresses

Tourism Malaysia, 17th Floor, Menara Dato'Onn, Putra World Trade Centre (PWTC), 45 Jalan Tun Ismail, 50480 Kuala Lumpur, Malaysia, tel: 603 2615 8188, e-mail: enquiries@tourism.gov.my website: www.tourism malaysia.gov.my

Sabah Tourism Board, 51 Gaya Street, 88000 Kota Kinabalu, Sabah, tel: 6088 212 121, e-mail: info@sabah tourism.com website: www.sabahtourism.com

Sabah Parks, Lot 1-3 Block K/ G Floor, Sinsuran Complex, Kota Kinabalu, Sabah, tel: 6088 211 881 e-mail: info@sabah parks.org.my website: www.sabahparks.org.my

Sabah Wildlife Department, 5th Floor, B Block, Wisma MUIS, 88100 Kota Kinabalu, Sabah, tel: 6088 215 353, e-mail: jhlsabah@tm.net.my website: www.sabah.gov.my

Sarawak Tourism Board, 6th & 7the Floor, Bangunan Yayasan Sarawak, Jalan Masjid, 93400 Kuching, Sarawak, tel: 6082 423 600, e-mail: stb@sarawaktourism.com website: www.sarawak tourism.com

National Park Booking Office (For Permits), Visitor Information Centre, Jalan Tun Abang Haji Openg, 93000 Kuching, Sarawak, tel: 6082 248 088, fax: 6082 248 087.

General Advice

When visiting Malaysian national parks, wildlife reserves and marine parks, it is advisable to keep informed of the rules and regulations of the park authority, particularly if you are camping, trekking and mountain climbing. It is strictly forbidden to remove any plants or corals or cause disturbance to the wildlife. All nature and park guides are professionally trained in their field and it would be wise to follow their

Travel Tips

advice, especially when out trekking on jungle trails or exploring caves where there might be natural hazards.

Health Requirements

Wildlife parks in the Malaysian wilderness have challenges like snakes, insects and leeches as well as other hazards of the wild. It is advisable to seek medical advice from your doctor in your home country before embarking on your journey, particularly with regard to anti-malarial medicine and antidotes for wasp or bee stings if you suffer from such an allergy. Avoid walking in long grass with bare feet or in sandals or shorts. If bitten by a poisonous snake or other venomous creature, try to identify it for treatment purposes. When staying in jungle lodges or camping, check for spiders or scorpions inside your shoes before putting them on. Travel and health insurance is compulsory if you are planning to participate in activities such as scuba diving, cave exploration and jungle trekking; make sure these activities are covered in your insurance policies.

Health Services

In most major cities, medical centres offer the best health service. Private clinics are available even in small towns. There are government hospitals throughout the country but they are more geared to the needs of the local population. Pharmacies dispensing western as well as Chinese traditional medicine are found mainly in department stores and supermarkets. For up-to-date information on health matters affecting Malaysia, see www.masta.org and www.tmb.ie

Emergencies

Dial 999 for police, ambulance or fire.

Entry Documents

All foreign visitors to Malaysia must be in possession of valid national passports or travel documents recognized by the Malaysian Government. Such passport or travel documents must be valid for at least six months beyond the period of stay permitted in Malaysia. Most bona fide visitors are automatically granted a 30-day or 60-day permit upon arrival in Malaysia. The states of Sarawak and Sabah have their own immigration control, but most nationalities are granted the same length of stay as in Peninsular Malaysia upon arrival. However, visitors from some countries may require visas and if you are in doubt, check with the Malaysian Embassy in your home countries or check on www.imi.gov.my – the official website of the Immigration Department of Malaysia.

Language

The official language of Malaysia is Bahasa Melayu (Malay), but English is widely spoken – even in some remote areas – and it is also used in commerce, trade and the media.

Religion

The official religion of Malaysia is Islam but there is freedom of worship for every religion.

Electricity

Mains voltage is 220 volts and three-pin plugs are used.

Time

Malaysian Standard Time is eight hours ahead of Greenwich Mean Time (Universal Standard Time), seven hours ahead of Central European Winter Time, and 13 hours ahead of the USA's Eastern Standard Winter Time.

Important Notice: Trafficking In Illegal Drugs Carries The Death Penalty In Malaysia.

Selected Animal and Bird Gallery

Clouded Leopard

Asian Elephant

Bearded Pig

Sumatran Rhinoceros

Barking Deer

Sun Bear

Wild Boar

Malayan Tapir

Panther

Common Palm Civet

Banded Palm Civet

Bay Cat

Lesser Mousedeer

Short-tailed Mongoose

Marbled Cat

Sambar

Binturong (Bearcat)

Malayan Tiger

Asiatic Brushtailed Porcupine

Pangolin

Slow Loris

Hairy-nosed Otter

Malayan Flying Lemur

Western Tarsier

Yellow-throated Marten

Oriental Small-clawed Otter

Animals

Slender Squirrel

Black Giant Squirrel

Plantain Squirrel

Red Giant Flying Squirrel

Grey-bellied Squirrel

Siamang

Pig-tailed Macaque

White-handed Gibbon

Banded Leaf Monkey

Silvered Leaf Monkey

Orang-utan

Proboscis Monkey

Bornean Gibbon

Long-tailed Macaque

Skink (Sun Lizard)

Common Water Monitor

Green Crested Lizard

Estuarine Crocodile

Yellow-ringed Cat Snake

Wagler's Pit Viper

Reticulated Python

Hawksbill Turtle

Spiny Hill Turtle

Green Turtle

Selected Animal and Bird Gallery

Asian Glossy Starling

Banded Bay Cuckoo

Black-and-Red Broadbill

Asian Fairy Bluebird

Black-and-Yellow Broadbill

Black-crested Bulbul

Black-headed Munia

Black-shouldered Kite

Black-thighed Falconet

Blue-banded Kingfisher

Blue-breasted Quail

Blue-crowned Hanging Parrot

Blue-tailed Bee-eater

Blue-throated Bee-eater

Blue-winged Pitta

Buffy Fish-Owl

Changeable Hawk-Eagle

Chestnut-breasted Malkoha

Chestnut-capped Laughingthrush

Chestnut-crowned Laughingthrush

Birds

Chestnut-necklaced Partridge

Cinnamon-rumped Trogon

Collared Kingfisher

Common Green Magpie

Common Tailorbird

Crested Goshawk

Crested Serpent Eagle

Dusky Broadbill

Fiery Minivet

Golden-throated Barbet

Gold-whiskered Barbet

Greater Racquet-tailed Drongo

Little Heron

Grey-faced Buzzard

Spangled Drongo

Green Broadbill

Large-tailed Nightjar

House Swift

Lesser Green Leafbird

Lesser Racquet-tailed Drongo

Selected Animal and Bird Gallery

Mountain Imperial
Pigeon

Long-billed Partridge

Maroon
Woodpecker

Rufous
Woodpecker

Mountain Tailorbird

Oriental Magpie Robin

Oriental Pied
Hornbill

Oriental
Plover

Pacific Swallow

Peregrine Falcon

Pied Harrier

Pied Triller

Pink-necked Green
Pigeon

Plaintive
Cuckoo

Purple Heron

Red Junglefowl

Red-throated Sunbird

White-headed Munia

Richard's Pipit

Ruddy Kingfisher

Birds

Little Ringed Plover

Rufous-collared
Kingfisher

Rusty-breasted
Cuckoo

Scarlet-backed
Flowerpecker

Sooty-capped Babbler

Hill Myna

Spectacled
Spiderhunter

Storm's Stork

Violet Cuckoo

Whiskered Treeswift

White-bellied Sea Eagle

White-breasted Waterhen

Yellow-bellied Bulbul

Yellow Bittern

White-crowned
Hornbill

Rhinoceros
Hornbill

White-rumped Shama

Wrinkled Hornbill

Wreathed Hornbill

Great Argus

Check list

Top Mammals
- ☐☐ Asian Elephant
- ☐☐ Asiatic Brush-tailed Porcupine
- ☐☐ Banded Leaf Monkey
- ☐☐ Banded Palm Civet
- ☐☐ Barking Deer
- ☐☐ Bay Cat
- ☐☐ Bearded Pig
- ☐☐ Binturong (Bearcat)
- ☐☐ Black Giant Squirrel
- ☐☐ Bornean Gibbon
- ☐☐ Clouded Leopard
- ☐☐ Common Palm Civet
- ☐☐ Grey-bellied Squirrel
- ☐☐ Hairy-nosed Otter
- ☐☐ Lesser Mousedeer
- ☐☐ Long-tailed Macaque
- ☐☐ Malayan Flying Lemur
- ☐☐ Malayan Tapir
- ☐☐ Marbled Cat
- ☐☐ Orang-utan
- ☐☐ Oriental Small-clawed Otter
- ☐☐ Pangolin
- ☐☐ Panther
- ☐☐ Pig-tailed Macaque
- ☐☐ Plantain Squirrel
- ☐☐ Proboscis Monkey
- ☐☐ Red Giant Flying Squirrel
- ☐☐ Sambar
- ☐☐ Short-tailed Mongoose
- ☐☐ Siamang
- ☐☐ Silvered Leaf Monkey
- ☐☐ Slender Squirrel
- ☐☐ Slow Loris
- ☐☐ Sumatran Rhinoceros
- ☐☐ Sun Bear
- ☐☐ Tiger (Malayan Tiger)
- ☐☐ Western Tarsier
- ☐☐ White-handed Gibbon
- ☐☐ Wild Boar
- ☐☐ Yellow-throated Marten

Top Reptiles
- ☐☐ Common Water Monitor
- ☐☐ Estuarine Crocodile
- ☐☐ Green Turtle
- ☐☐ Green-crested Lizard
- ☐☐ Hawksbill Turtle
- ☐☐ Reticulated Python
- ☐☐ Skink (Sun Lizard)
- ☐☐ Spiny Hill Turtle
- ☐☐ Wagler's Pit Viper
- ☐☐ Yellow-ringed Cat Snake

Top Birds
- ☐☐ Asian Fairy Bluebird
- ☐☐ Asian Glossy Starling
- ☐☐ Asian Paradise Flycatcher
- ☐☐ Banded Bay Cuckoo
- ☐☐ Black Bittern
- ☐☐ Black Eagle
- ☐☐ Black-and-Red Broadbill
- ☐☐ Black-and-Yellow Broadbill
- ☐☐ Black-crested Bulbul
- ☐☐ Black-headed Munia
- ☐☐ Black-naped Oriole
- ☐☐ Black-shouldered Kite
- ☐☐ Black-thighed Falconet
- ☐☐ Blue-banded Kingfisher
- ☐☐ Blue-breasted Quail
- ☐☐ Blue-crowned Hanging Parrot
- ☐☐ Blue-tailed Bee-eater
- ☐☐ Blue-throated Bee-eater
- ☐☐ Blue-winged Pitta
- ☐☐ Bornean Barbet
- ☐☐ Brahminy Kite
- ☐☐ Buffy Fish-Owl
- ☐☐ Cattle Egret
- ☐☐ Changeable Hawk-Eagle
- ☐☐ Chestnut-breasted Malkoha

Check list

- ☐☐ Chestnut-capped Laughingthrush
- ☐☐ Chestnut-crowned Laughingthrush
- ☐☐ Chestnut-necklaced Partridge
- ☐☐ Cinnamon-rumped Trogon
- ☐☐ Collared Kingfisher
- ☐☐ Common Green Magpie
- ☐☐ Common Iora
- ☐☐ Common Tailorbird
- ☐☐ Crested Goshawk
- ☐☐ Crested Serpent Eagle
- ☐☐ Curlew Sandpiper
- ☐☐ Dusky Broadbill
- ☐☐ Fiery Minivet
- ☐☐ Golden-throated Barbet
- ☐☐ Gold-whiskered Barbet
- ☐☐ Great Argus
- ☐☐ Great Egret
- ☐☐ Greater Racquet-tailed Drongo
- ☐☐ Green Broadbill
- ☐☐ Green-winged Pigeon
- ☐☐ Grey-capped Woodpecker

- ☐☐ Grey-faced Buzzard
- ☐☐ Grey-headed Flycatcher
- ☐☐ Hill Myna
- ☐☐ House Swift
- ☐☐ Large-tailed Nightjar
- ☐☐ Lesser Green Leafbird
- ☐☐ Lesser Racquet-tailed Drongo
- ☐☐ Lesser Whistling Duck
- ☐☐ Little Cuckoo Dove
- ☐☐ Little Heron
- ☐☐ Little Ringed Plover
- ☐☐ Long-billed Partridge
- ☐☐ Maroon Woodpecker
- ☐☐ Mountain Imperial Pigeon
- ☐☐ Mountain Tailorbird
- ☐☐ Olive Tree-Pipit
- ☐☐ Oriental Darter
- ☐☐ Oriental Dwarf Kingfisher
- ☐☐ Oriental Magpie Robin
- ☐☐ Oriental Pied Hornbill
- ☐☐ Oriental Plover
- ☐☐ Pacific Swallow
- ☐☐ Peregrine Falcon
- ☐☐ Pied Harrier
- ☐☐ Pied Triller
- ☐☐ Pink-necked Green Pigeon
- ☐☐ Plaintive Cuckoo

- ☐☐ Purple Heron
- ☐☐ Red Junglefowl
- ☐☐ Red-throated Sunbird
- ☐☐ Rhinoceros Hornbill
- ☐☐ Richard's Pipit
- ☐☐ Ruddy Kingfisher
- ☐☐ Rufous Woodpecker
- ☐☐ Rufous-collared Kingfisher
- ☐☐ Rusty-breasted Cuckoo
- ☐☐ Scarlet-backed Flowerpecker
- ☐☐ Sooty-capped Babbler
- ☐☐ Spangled Drongo
- ☐☐ Spectacled Spiderhunter
- ☐☐ Storm's Stork
- ☐☐ Violet Cuckoo
- ☐☐ Whiskered Treeswift
- ☐☐ White-bellied Sea Eagle
- ☐☐ White-breasted Waterhen
- ☐☐ White-crowned Hornbill
- ☐☐ White-crowned Shama
- ☐☐ White-headed Munia
- ☐☐ White-rumped Shama
- ☐☐ Wreathed Hornbill
- ☐☐ Wrinkled Hornbill
- ☐☐ Yellow Bittern
- ☐☐ Yellow-bellied Bulbul
- ☐☐ Yellow-bellied Prinia
- ☐☐ Yellow-vented Bulbul

Index

Note: page numbers in **bold**
indicate photographs.

accommodation 38–39, 49, 57,
  65, 69, 84, 89, 101, 107,
  111–112, 117, 124–125, 135,
  141
adventure caving 82
agamid lizard **50**
Amorphophallus 79

Bako National Park **6**, 58, 60–65
Banjaran Titiwangsa 16
banteng 116 (see *also* wild cattle)
Batang Ai Lake **90**
Batang Ai National Park 92–101
beaches **142**
bearded pigs **22**, 107
Bebiyong Trail, Batang Ai
  National Park 98
Belitong Trail, Batang Ai National
  Park 99
Berawan people 81
birds 13, 17, 24–25, 96–98,
  152–155
bird-watching 85
boats **26**, **37**, **40**, **90**, **118**
Bornean bearded pigs see
  bearded pigs
Borneo Eco Tours 125
Borneo pygmy elephant **102**,
  110
Borneo Rainforest Lodge **102**,
  107
Brahminy Kite **99**
Buaya Sangkut 44
Bukit Kasut Trail, Niah National
  Park 89
Bukit Teresek 33

Cameron Highlands **6**
camp sites 44
Canopy Walkway, Taman
  Negara National Park
  32, **33**
check list 156–157
Clearwater Cave 81
climate 10, 17
climbing Mount Kinabalu
  132–135
clouded leopards 20
clown fish **136**

Danum Valley Conservation
  Area 104–108
dawn river safari 123
dawn safari **118**
Deer Cave 79–80
diving at Sipadan Island
  138
dolphins 60
Donkey's Ears, Mount Kinabalu
  128, **134**
drugs 149
dusky leaf monkey **18**

electricity 149
elephants 19 (see *also* Borneo
  pygmy elephant)
emergencies 149
Endau River 41
Endau Rompin National Park
  40–49, **40**, **45**
Enggam Trail, Batang Ai National
  Park 100
entry documents 149
estuarine crocodile **118**

fauna 87, 93–96, 130, 141
Fire Mountain see Gunung Api
fishing 46
flora 86, 98, 130, 141
flora and fauna 28–30, 32–33
forest types 11–16
free-tailed bats 80

getting there 37, 48, 57, 65, 68,
  69, 84, 89, 101, 106, 111, 116,
  124, 127, 141
Gomantong Caves 123
Great Cave Trail, Niah National
  Park 87
Great Cave, Niah **76**
green turtle **142**
Gua Telinga 35
Gunung Api **76**, 82
Gunung Gading National Park
  69
Gunung Mulu 17
Gunung Mulu National Park
  78–84
Gunung Tahan 17, 36

head-hunting 82
health 149

Heart of Borneo Declaration
  143
Hilton Batang Ai Longhouse
  Resort **90**, 95

independent travel 100
islands
  Langkawi 8
  Pangkor Laut 8, 18
  Perhentian **142**
  Redang 8
  Sipadan Island **136**, 138–140
  Tioman 8

jackfruit **15**
Jasin River **45**
jungle expeditions 32, 43
jungle hide **31**

Kinabalu National Park 128–135,
  128
Kinabatangan River **118**
Kinabatangan Wildlife Sanctuary
  120–125
Krau Wildlife Reserve 147
Kuala Lumpur 10
Kuala Sungai Tahan **26**
Kuala Tahan **26**
Kubah National Park 65–69

Lambir Hills National Park **142**,
  143
Lang's Cave 80
Langkawi 8
language 35, 149
langurs 22
Lanjak Entimau Wildlife
  Sanctuary 91
Lata Berkoh **34**
leeches 39
leopards 20
limestone pinnacles of Gunung
  Api 82–83
Lipad Mud Volcano 114, **115**
Loagan Bunut National Park 144
longhouses of Sarawak 92
long-tailed macaque **88**
Low's Gully **128**

Madu Trail, Niah National Park
  88
Malayan flying lemur **62**

Index

Malayan tiger **55**, 57
Malaysian states 10
Maliau Basin 108–112
mammals 14, 19, 150–151
marine life 140
Matang Wildlife Centre, Kubah National Park 67
megabat flying foxes **76**
monitor lizards **58**
monkeys 22
montane forest **128**
Mount Kinabalu 17, **128**
mountain climbing 133
mountains
  Banjaran Titiwangsa 16
  Gunung Mulu 17
  Gunung Tahan 17, 36
  Kinabalu 17, **128**
mudskipper **58**
Mulu Caves 18
Mussaenda mutabilis **46**

Niah Caves 86–87
Niah National Park **76**, 84–89
night safari 32, 115

Orang Asli people **37**, 55–56
Orang Asli settlements 36, 45
orang-utan 22, 74–75, **75**, **118**, **124**
orchids 73, **83**, **109**

Painted Cave 88
Palmarium trail, Kubah National Park **65**
Pangkor Laut 8, 18
pangolin 63
Park Authority Information 29
park fees 47
park regulations 47, 130
Pedalai Trail, Batang Ai National Park 98
Penang National Park 144
Perhentian **142**
Perlis State Park 147
pigs 22
pitcher plant **72**
Pitcher Plant and Wild Orchid Centre, Kuching 73
porcupine **56**
proboscis monkey **23**
Pulau Kalumpunian Damit **136**

Pulau Payar Marine Park 145
Pulau Perhentian 146
Pulau Redang Marine Park 146
Pulau Tiga National Park 140–141
Pulau Tioman Marine Park **6**, 146

Rafflesia **70**, 70–71
rainforest 11, **105**
Rajang River 17
raspberries **133**
Redang Island 8
religion 149
reptiles 16, 20, 151
rhinoceros 20 (*see also* Sumatran rhinoceros)
rhinoceros beetle **49**
Rhinoceros Hornbill **97**
river safari 121
rivers
  Endau 41
  Jasin **45**
  Kinabatangan **118**
  Rajang 17
  Rompin 41
  Sungai Jasin 41
  Sungai Selai 41
Royal Belum State Park **50**, 50–57
Rumah Chang, Niah National Park 89

Sabah 104
Sabah Foundation 112
safety on a canopy walk 32
sambar deer **28**
Sandakan 120
saving the rhino 116
sea anemones **136**
sea krait **136**
seladang see wild cattle
Semenggoh Wildlife Centre 68
Sepilok Mangrove Forest Trail 126
Sepilok Orang-utan Rehabilitation Centre 17, 125–127
shooting the rapids 36
silvered leaf monkey **121**

Similajau National Park 143
Singalang Burung see Brahminy Kite
Sipadan Island **136**, 138–140
Sium Trail, Batang Ai National Park 100
slow loris **94**
spotted litter frog **40**
Sumatran rhinoceros 21, **117**
Sungai Endau **40**
Sungai Jasin 41, **45**
Sungai Selai 41
Sungai Tembeling **26**
survival kit 8

Tabin Wildlife Reserve **102**, 113–116
Tabin Wildlife Reserve Lodge 116
Taman Negara National Park 26–39, **33**, **38**
Tanjong Datu National Park 143
Tanjung Piai National Park 145
tapirs 20
Temengor Forest Reserve 50–57
Temengor Lake **50**
tigers 20 (*see also* Malayan tiger)
time 149
Tioman 8
tour companies 134, 148
travel tips 148–149
Trichoglottis smithii **109**
Tunku Abdul Rahman National Park 145
Turtle Islands Marine Park 145

Upeh Guling Falls 45
useful contacts 38, 101, 148
useful information 48, 135

White-bellied Sea Eagle **24**
White-throated Kingfisher **25**
wild cattle 19
wildlife 18–19, 106
Wind Cave 81

Imprint Page

First edition published in 2008
by New Holland Publishers (UK) Ltd
London • Cape Town • Sydney • Auckland
10 9 8 7 6 5 4 3 2 1

website: www.newhollandpublishers.com

Garfield House, 86 Edgware Road
London W2 2EA, United Kingdom

80 McKenzie Street
Cape Town 8001, South Africa

Unit 1, 66 Gibbes Street
Chatswood, NSW 2067, Australia

218 Lake Road, Northcote
Auckland, New Zealand

Distributed in the USA by
The Globe Pequot Press, Connecticut

This guidebook has been written by independent authors
and updaters. The information therein represents their
impartial opinion, and neither they nor the publishers
accept payment in return for including in the book or
writing more favourable reviews of any of the establish-
ments. Whilst every effort has been made to ensure that
this guidebook is as accurate and up to date as possible,
please be aware that the facts quoted are subject to
change, particularly the price of food, transport and
accommodation. The Publisher accepts no responsibility
or liability for any loss, injury or inconvenience incurred
by readers or travellers using this guide.

Keep us Current
Information in travel guides is apt to change, which is
why we regularly update our guides. We'd be grateful to
receive feedback if you've noted something we should
include in our updates. If you have new information,
please share it with us by writing to the Publishing
Manager, Globetrotter, at the office nearest to you
(addresses on this page). The most significant contribu-
tion to each new edition will receive a free copy of the
updated guide.

Publishing Manager: Thea Grobbelaar
DTP Cartographic Manager: Genené Hart
Editor: Thea Grobbelaar
Design and DTP: Beverley Dodd
Cover Design: Nicole Bannister
Cartographer: Tanja Spinola
Picture Researchers: Shavonne Govender,
Zainoenisa Manuel
Consultants: Rick Gregory, Ken Scriven
Proofreader: Nicky Steenkamp
Illustrators: Richard Allen, Tim Worfolk, Stephen
Message, Jan Wilczur, Clive Byers, Mike Langman, Ian
Lewington, Christopher Schmidt, Andrew Mackay, John
Cox, Anthony Disley, Hilary Burn, Daniel Cole and
Martin Elliott (birds);
Steven Felmore (mammals and reptiles)

Reproduction by Resolution, Cape Town
Printed and bound in China by C & C Offset Printing
Co., Ltd.

Acknowledgments: The author wishes to thank the
Sarawak Tourism Board for their help with this project.

Photographic credits:
Andrew Bannister: pages 6 (top), 15, 26 (centre),
28, 31, 33, 34, 37, 38, 58 (top and bottom), 72, 83,
97, 128 (top, centre and bottom), 136 (top), 142
(centre and bottom); **David Bowden:** back cover
(top), page 102 (bottom); **Andy Craggs:** front
cover; **Gerald Cubitt:** back cover (centre and
bottom), pages 1, 6 (centre and bottom), 18, 21, 22,
24, 25, 26 (top and bottom), 40 (top and bottom), 45,
46, 49, 50 (top, centre and bottom), 55, 56, 62, 65,
70, 76 (top and centre), 90 (bottom), 94, 99, 102
(centre), 105, 109, 115, 117, 118 (top, centre and
bottom), 121, 133, 134, 136 (centre), 142 (top);
Nicholas Gill: page 58 (centre); **Rick Gregory:**
page 40 (centre); **Hilton Batang Ai Longhouse
Resort:** page 90 (top and centre); **Anne Kartz:**
pages 23, 88; **Robin Lane/Images of Africa:** page
136 (bottom); **Kwan Fah Mun:** page 102 (top);
SARAWAK FORESTRY: pages 4–5, 75, 76
(bottom), 124; **Tabin Wildlife Resort:** pages 2–3.

Cover: *An orang-utan in Borneo (front); Lake Kenyir,
a dusky leaf monkey in the forests of Penang Hill, a
rhinoceros hornbill in Sarawak (back, top to bottom).*
Half title page: *A tapir, Taman Negara.*
Title page: *A group of pygmy elephants.*
Contents page: *Pinnacles at Gunung Mulu.*